STOCK MARKET CRASH

by

Lalit Mohanty

PREFACE

The stock market has long been a symbol of wealth creation, a place where fortunes are made and lost in equal measure. Yet, for all its potential rewards, the market is also a source of profound anxiety, especially during turbulent times. When the market crashes, the noise of panic often drowns out the voice of reason, leaving many investors feeling paralyzed, vulnerable, and uncertain about the future.

This book was born out of a desire to provide clarity amidst the chaos. Having observed and studied market behavior for years, I've seen firsthand how the same patterns repeat during every crash: fear takes over, mistakes are made, and opportunities are missed. But I've also witnessed how informed and disciplined investors can turn these crises into moments of incredible opportunity.

In *Stock Market Crash*, my goal is to empower you with the knowledge and mindset needed to navigate market downturns with confidence. From understanding the root causes of crashes to avoiding common mistakes, from recognizing the role of emotions to implementing proven strategies for success, this book is a comprehensive guide for anyone who wants to thrive, not just survive, in the face of market adversity.

I've taken care to include lessons from history, real-world examples, and actionable insights that can help investors at all levels—whether you're just starting out or have years of experience. Above all, this book is about shifting your perspective: seeing a crash not as an end, but as a beginning; not as a loss, but as a chance to rebuild smarter and stronger.

As you read, I encourage you to approach the market with patience, discipline, and a sense of curiosity. The journey to becoming a resilient investor is not without its challenges, but the rewards of mastering this skill go far beyond financial gain.

Thank you for allowing me to share this journey with you. Together, let's prepare for the next market downturn—not with fear, but with a strategy.

Lalit Prasad Mohant

Table of Contents

Introduction:

- Define a stock market crash and its causes.
- Brief historical perspective on major crashes (e.g., 1929, 1987, 2008, 2020).
- The emotional and financial impact of market downturns on investors.

Chapter 1: The Anatomy of a Stock Market Crash

- Factors that trigger crashes (economic bubbles, geopolitical tensions, etc.).
- How fear and panic exacerbate downturns.
- The role of institutional investors and algorithmic trading.

Chapter 2: Common Mistakes Investors Make During a Crash

- Selling in panic.
- Checking portfolios excessively and making impulsive decisions.

- Following the crowd or "herd mentality."
- Over-leveraging or holding non-diversified portfolios.

Chapter 3: The Psychology of a Crash

- Understanding fear, loss aversion, and other cognitive biases.
- How to build emotional resilience as an investor.

Chapter 4: How to React During a Crash

- Practical steps to assess your financial situation.
- The importance of a long-term perspective.
- Strategies for portfolio rebalancing and damage control.

Chapter 5: Turning a Crisis into an Opportunity

- Identifying undervalued stocks and sectors.
- Dollar-cost averaging during market lows.
- Learning from Warren Buffett's approach to market downturns.

Chapter 6: Lessons from Historical Crashes

- Case studies of companies and investors who emerged stronger.
- Patterns and insights from past recoveries.

Chapter 7: Building a Crash-Resilient Portfolio

- The importance of diversification and asset allocation.
- Hedging strategies using options, gold, or bonds.

- Emergency funds and liquidity management.

Chapter 8: Timing the Market: Myth or Reality?

- Why it's almost impossible to predict a crash accurately.
- The dangers of trying to time the market versus staying invested.

Chapter 9: Strategies for Profiting During and After a Crash

- Short selling: risks and rewards.
- Buying high-quality stocks at a discount.
- Investing in ETFs and index funds post-crash.

Chapter 10: Preparing for the Next Crash

- Recognizing red flags in the market.
- Building a solid investment plan with contingencies.
- Educating yourself continuously about market trends.

INTRODUCTION

The stock market is often referred to as the heartbeat of an economy, reflecting its growth, potential, and stability. Yet, like the human heart, it is prone to sudden jolts that disrupt its rhythm. These jolts, which we call stock market crashes, can have profound and far-reaching effects—not only on the financial system but also on individual investors, businesses, and governments.

A **stock market crash** is a rapid and often unexpected decline in stock prices across a significant portion of the market. This sharp drop, usually marked by a decline of 20% or more from recent highs, is driven by a combination of fear, uncertainty, and selling pressure that spreads like wildfire. Unlike a market correction, which is a normal part of stock market cycles and typically temporary, a crash often signals deeper issues within the economy or financial system.

Crashes evoke images of chaos: brokers shouting on trading floors, financial news channels broadcasting plummeting charts, and investors frantically checking their portfolios. But beneath the visible panic lies a complex web of causes that ignite and fuel these crises.

Causes of a Stock Market Crash

1. **Economic Bubbles and Overvaluation**
   A common precursor to a crash is the formation of an economic bubble, where the prices of assets, particularly stocks, become detached from their intrinsic value. Driven by speculation and herd behavior, investors pour money into these overvalued assets, creating unsustainable highs. Eventually, the bubble bursts, and prices fall dramatically. Notable examples include the Dot-com Bubble of the late 1990s and the Housing Bubble of 2008.

2. **Global or Economic Shocks**
   External events like geopolitical tensions, wars, pandemics, or natural disasters can create uncertainty and lead to abrupt market declines. For instance, the COVID-19 pandemic in early 2020 triggered a sharp global market selloff as economies came to a standstill.

3. **Financial System Vulnerabilities**
   Structural weaknesses within the financial system, such as excessive debt, lack of regulation, or systemic risks from large institutions, can amplify the impact of a downturn. The collapse of Lehman Brothers in 2008 is a striking example of how interconnectedness within the financial system can accelerate a crash.

4. **Mass Psychology and Panic Selling**
   Human behavior plays a significant role in crashes. When investors lose confidence, fear spreads rapidly. Panic selling, where investors rush to offload stocks at any price, drives the market lower and triggers a self-reinforcing downward spiral.

5. **High Levels of Leverage**
   Leverage amplifies gains in rising markets but becomes a ticking time bomb during downturns. When markets fall, heavily leveraged investors are forced to sell assets to cover losses, further driving down prices.

6. **Technological Factors**
   In today's world of high-frequency trading and algorithmic systems, crashes can be accelerated by technology. The 2010 Flash Crash demonstrated how automated systems could amplify volatility, causing prices to plummet in seconds.

7. **Interest Rate and Monetary Policy Changes**
   Sudden shifts in central bank policies, such as raising interest rates, can make borrowing more expensive and reduce corporate profits. This often leads to a decline in stock prices as investors anticipate slower economic growth.

The Ripple Effect of a Crash

The consequences of a stock market crash extend beyond Wall Street. Businesses may struggle to secure funding, leading to layoffs and reduced consumer spending. Retirement accounts, often tied to stock market performance, lose value, causing widespread financial anxiety. Governments may step in with stimulus measures, but recovery is often slow and painful.

However, it's important to recognize that crashes are an inherent part of the market's cycle. Just as economies experience periods of growth and contraction, the stock market follows a similar pattern of booms and busts. What distinguishes successful investors is their ability to understand these cycles, manage their emotions, and act strategically during downturns.

This book will guide you through the complexities of stock market crashes, exploring not only their causes but also the strategies you can employ to safeguard your investments and seize opportunities that arise in the chaos. By understanding the mechanics of a crash, you'll be better equipped to navigate the inevitable storms of the financial markets.

Brief Historical Perspective on Major Stock Market Crashes

Throughout history, stock market crashes have served as dramatic reminders of the financial system's vulnerabilities. Each crash has its own story, shaped by unique circumstances, but they all share common themes of speculation, fear, and economic turmoil. Here, we will explore four of the most significant crashes: the Great Crash of 1929, Black Monday of 1987, the Global Financial Crisis of 2008, and the COVID-19 Crash of 2020.

The Great Crash of 1929

- **Timeline:** October 24, 1929 (Black Thursday) to late 1930s
- **Key Causes:** Speculation, excessive leverage, and lack of regulation.
- **Impact:** The Great Depression, with global economic fallout.

The stock market boom of the 1920s was fueled by a wave of optimism and speculative trading, as investors believed the market would rise indefinitely. However, this confidence was built on shaky foundations: stocks were significantly overvalued, and many investors purchased them on margin (borrowed money). When the bubble burst, panic selling ensued.

Black Thursday (October 24, 1929) marked the beginning of the crash, with the Dow Jones Industrial Average (DJIA) dropping 11% in a single day. By October 29, known as Black Tuesday, the market had plummeted even further, wiping out billions of dollars in wealth.

The aftermath was catastrophic: the Great Depression, marked by widespread unemployment, deflation, and economic stagnation, lasted for a decade. The 1929 crash highlighted the need for regulatory reforms, leading to the creation of the Securities and Exchange Commission (SEC) in the United States.

Black Monday: 1987

- **Timeline:** October 19, 1987
- **Key Causes:** Program trading, overvaluation, and lack of market safeguards.
- **Impact:** Global market panic but a swift recovery.

On October 19, 1987, the stock market experienced its largest single-day percentage drop in history. The DJIA fell by 22.6%, equivalent to a modern-day drop of over 7,000 points. The causes were multifaceted, including the use of program trading—computer-driven strategies that automatically triggered massive sell-offs as prices declined.

Black Monday sent shockwaves across global markets, with similar crashes occurring in London, Hong Kong, and other financial hubs. While the crash caused widespread panic, its impact on the economy was relatively short-lived. Markets rebounded within months, thanks to coordinated interventions by central banks and financial institutions.

This crash underscored the dangers of relying heavily on automated trading systems and the importance of circuit breakers to halt trading during extreme volatility.

The Global Financial Crisis: 2008

- **Timeline:** September 15, 2008, to early 2009
- **Key Causes:** Housing bubble collapse, subprime mortgage crisis, and financial system vulnerabilities.
- **Impact:** Recession, massive job losses, and global financial instability.

The 2008 crisis was triggered by the bursting of the U.S. housing bubble, fueled by risky subprime mortgages and complex financial instruments like mortgage-backed securities (MBS) and collateralized debt obligations (CDOs). When homeowners defaulted on their loans, the entire financial system, which was heavily exposed to these toxic assets, began to unravel.

Lehman Brothers, one of the largest investment banks, filed for bankruptcy on September 15, 2008, marking a turning point in the crisis. Stock markets worldwide tumbled, with the DJIA losing more than 50% of its value from its peak. Major financial institutions required government bailouts to prevent total collapse.

The aftermath included a global recession, with millions losing their homes, jobs, and savings. Governments responded with massive stimulus packages and reforms, such as the Dodd-Frank Act, to prevent a repeat of such a catastrophic failure.

The COVID-19 Crash: 2020

- **Timeline:** February to March 2020
- **Key Causes:** Pandemic-driven economic shutdown and panic.
- **Impact:** Short-term recession and rapid recovery.

The COVID-19 pandemic brought the world to a standstill in early 2020. As the virus spread and governments imposed lockdowns, economic activity ground to a halt. Investors panicked, leading to a swift and steep decline in stock prices.

Between February 20 and March 23, 2020, the S&P 500 dropped nearly 34%, marking one of the fastest bear markets in history. Unlike previous crashes, the COVID-19 crash was not caused by financial system flaws or economic imbalances but by an unprecedented health crisis.

However, the recovery was equally dramatic. Central banks and governments worldwide responded with aggressive monetary and fiscal policies, including near-zero interest rates and massive stimulus packages. By the end of 2020, markets had not only recovered but reached new highs, driven by optimism about vaccines and economic reopening.

Lessons from History

Each of these crashes teaches important lessons about the market's vulnerabilities and resilience:

- **1929** showed the dangers of unchecked speculation and the importance of regulation.
- **1987** highlighted the risks of overreliance on technology and the need for safeguards like circuit breakers.
- **2008** exposed systemic risks in financial markets and the need for better oversight.
- **2020** demonstrated the power of coordinated government action to stabilize markets.

Stock market crashes are inevitable, but understanding their causes and consequences can help investors navigate them with greater confidence and emerge stronger.

The Emotional and Financial Impact of Market Downturns on Investors

Stock market downturns are more than just numbers flashing red on a screen—they are events that profoundly affect investors both emotionally and financially. For many, these periods of turmoil bring intense feelings of fear, uncertainty, and even despair, often leading to rash decisions that can have long-term consequences. Understanding the emotional and financial toll of market downturns is essential for navigating these turbulent times with resilience and strategy.

The Emotional Impact of Market Downturns

1. **Fear and Panic**
   The immediate reaction to a sharp market decline is often fear. Investors worry about losing their hard-earned money, seeing their portfolios shrink, and the possibility of not being able to recover. This fear can escalate into panic, leading to impulsive actions such as selling off assets at the worst possible time.

During the 2008 financial crisis, many investors liquidated their holdings near market bottoms, only to miss out on the eventual recovery. Panic selling locks in losses and undermines long-term financial goals.

2. **Regret and Self-Doubt**
   As portfolios lose value, many investors begin questioning their decisions. Thoughts like *"Why didn't I sell earlier?"* or *"Why didn't I diversify more?"* can lead to regret and erode confidence in one's ability to manage finances effectively.

3. **Stress and Anxiety**
   Watching the market decline day after day can be overwhelming, especially for those heavily invested in equities or relying on their portfolio for income. Stress from financial uncertainty can spill into other aspects of life, affecting relationships, health, and overall well-being.

4. **Herd Mentality and Peer Pressure**
   Market downturns often amplify herd behavior. Seeing others sell their investments or hearing negative news from peers can pressure investors into following suit, even when their strategy calls for patience. This psychological phenomenon exacerbates market declines and prevents rational decision-making.

5. **Loss Aversion**
   Humans are wired to feel the pain of loss more acutely than the joy of gain. During a downturn, this bias makes it emotionally challenging to stay invested or even consider buying more shares at lower prices.

6. **Despair and Hopelessness**
   In severe crashes, when portfolios lose significant value, some investors may feel a sense of despair, believing their financial future is irreparably damaged. This emotional state can lead to inaction or, worse, abandoning investing altogether.

The Financial Impact of Market Downturns

1. **Portfolio Losses**
   The most immediate financial impact of a market downturn is the decline in the value of investments. For those nearing retirement or already retired, this can jeopardize plans, reduce income, and create anxiety about maintaining their standard of living.

2. **Reduction in Net Worth**
   For investors heavily reliant on equities, a crash can significantly reduce their net worth. This decline can affect access to loans, mortgages, and other financial resources tied to personal wealth.

3. **Forced Selling**
   Investors who are over-leveraged or lack sufficient liquidity may be forced to sell assets at unfavorable prices to meet margin calls or cover expenses. This locks in losses and leaves little room for recovery when markets rebound.

4. **Opportunity Costs**
   Those who sell during downturns often miss the opportunity to buy undervalued stocks or participate in the recovery. While some investors exit the market in panic, disciplined investors see crashes as opportunities to build wealth by buying quality assets at discounted prices.

5. **Impact on Retirement Plans**
   A downturn can disrupt long-term financial goals, particularly for individuals close to retirement. Losses in retirement accounts such as 401(k)s or IRAs may require delaying retirement, reducing planned spending, or adjusting financial goals.

6. **Income Disruption**
   Investors relying on dividend-paying stocks or investment income may face challenges during market downturns if companies cut or suspend dividends to preserve cash. This can affect monthly budgets and financial security.

7. **Broader Economic Effects**
   Severe market downturns often coincide with or contribute to economic recessions, leading to job losses, reduced consumer spending, and falling property values. This broader economic impact affects investors indirectly, even if their portfolios are relatively insulated.

The Interplay Between Emotional and Financial Impact

The emotional and financial effects of market downturns are deeply intertwined. Emotional responses such as fear and regret often lead to poor financial decisions, like panic selling or abandoning long-term plans. Conversely, financial losses exacerbate stress and anxiety, creating a vicious cycle that can be hard to break.

For example, during the 2020 COVID-19 crash, many investors saw their portfolios lose 30-40% of their value in just weeks. The emotional turmoil caused some to exit the market entirely, missing the subsequent recovery as markets surged to new highs by the end of the year.

How to Manage the Impact

1. **Emotional Discipline**
   - Acknowledge that market downturns are a natural part of investing.
   - Focus on long-term goals instead of short-term volatility.
   - Practice mindfulness or other stress-reduction techniques to stay calm during crises.

2. **Financial Preparedness**
   - Diversify investments to reduce exposure to market declines.
   - Maintain an emergency fund to avoid forced selling during downturns.
   - Rebalance portfolios periodically to align with risk tolerance.

3. **Educating Yourself**

- Learn from historical market crashes to understand recovery patterns.
- Seek advice from financial professionals or trusted resources to make informed decisions.

4. **Adopting a Long-Term Perspective**
    - Recognize that every major downturn in history has eventually been followed by a recovery.
    - Use market declines as opportunities to buy high-quality assets at discounted prices.

Market downturns, while challenging, are an integral part of the investment journey. By understanding the emotional and financial impacts, you can better prepare yourself to navigate these turbulent times with confidence and turn adversity into opportunity.

CHAPTER 1

THE ANATOMY OF A STOCK MARKET CRASH

The stock market, often a symbol of prosperity and economic health, can sometimes crumble in a matter of days, erasing fortunes and shaking the foundations of global economies. To truly understand the dynamics of these crashes, we need to dissect their anatomy—examining what triggers them, how they unfold, and their profound impact on individuals, businesses, and nations.

Understanding Stock Market Crashes

A stock market crash occurs when the prices of stocks plummet rapidly, often accompanied by panic selling and a sharp decline in investor confidence. While market corrections—a drop of 10% or more—are considered healthy and part of a normal market cycle, crashes are extreme events where the market loses significant value over a very short period.

What makes a crash particularly damaging is its ripple effect. A plunge in the market can lead to diminished investor confidence, widespread financial losses, and, in severe cases, economic recessions. But crashes don't happen in isolation. They are the result of a combination of factors, building over time until a tipping point is reached.

Factors That Trigger Stock Market Crashes

1. Economic Bubbles and Irrational Exuberance

One of the most common precursors to a stock market crash is the formation of economic bubbles. These bubbles occur when asset prices rise far beyond their intrinsic value, fueled by speculative buying and unrealistic expectations of future growth.

- **Example: The Dot-Com Bubble (2000)** During the late 1990s, internet-related companies saw their valuations skyrocket as investors poured money into any company with a ".com" in its name. With little regard for profitability or sustainable business models, this frenzy led to a massive bubble. When reality set in, and investors realized these companies could not deliver on their lofty promises, the bubble burst, wiping out trillions in market value.

Bubbles are fueled by **irrational exuberance**, a term popularized by economist Robert Shiller, referring to investor overconfidence and a herd mentality that drives prices to unsustainable levels.

2. Geopolitical Tensions and Global Uncertainty

Geopolitical events—wars, trade disputes, or political instability—can create uncertainty in financial markets, triggering a flight to safety. Investors sell risky assets like stocks in favor of safer options such as gold or government bonds.

- **Example: The 1990 Gulf War**
  When Iraq invaded Kuwait, oil prices surged, creating uncertainty in global markets. The stock market reacted with volatility, as investors feared the conflict would escalate and disrupt the global economy.

Similarly, ongoing trade wars or political unrest can lead to market crashes, as they affect global supply chains, trade agreements, and investor confidence.

3. Over-Leveraging and Margin Calls

Excessive borrowing, or leveraging, amplifies the impact of market downturns. Investors often use borrowed money to buy stocks, expecting prices to rise. However, when prices fall, lenders issue **margin calls**, requiring investors to sell assets to repay loans. This forced selling can create a downward spiral, further driving down stock prices.

- **Example: The 1929 Stock Market Crash**
  In the lead-up to the Great Depression, many investors bought stocks on margin, putting down as little as 10% of the purchase price and borrowing the rest. When the market began to decline, margin calls forced widespread selling, accelerating the crash.

4. Rapid Technological Changes and Algorithmic Trading

While technological advancements have improved market efficiency, they have also introduced new vulnerabilities. Algorithmic trading—where computer programs execute trades based on pre-set conditions—can exacerbate market downturns. During a crash, algorithms may trigger automated sell-offs, amplifying the speed and severity of the decline.

- **Example: The 2010 Flash Crash**
  On May 6, 2010, the Dow Jones Industrial Average plunged nearly 1,000 points within minutes before quickly recovering. This unprecedented event was attributed to a combination of human error and high-frequency trading algorithms, which created a feedback loop of rapid selling.

5. Economic Indicators and Weak Fundamentals

Crashes are often preceded by signs of economic weakness, such as:

- Declining corporate earnings
- High unemployment rates
- Slowing GDP growth
- Rising inflation or interest rates

When these indicators align with overvalued markets, they can serve as a warning that a correction—or crash—is imminent.

- **Example: The 2008 Financial Crisis**
  The collapse of Lehman Brothers was the catalyst for a global market crash, but the roots lay in weak economic fundamentals: a housing bubble fueled by subprime mortgages, lax regulatory oversight, and excessive risk-taking by financial institutions.

The Role of Investor Psychology

While economic and geopolitical factors set the stage for crashes, investor psychology often acts as the match that lights the fire. Fear and panic can spread like wildfire in a falling market, as investors rush to sell to avoid further losses. This herd mentality accelerates the decline, turning what might have been a correction into a full-blown crash.

- **Fear of Missing Out (FOMO):** Fuels bubbles during bull markets.
- **Fear of Loss:** Triggers panic selling during bear markets.

Understanding these psychological forces is crucial for navigating volatile markets.

The Domino Effect

A crash rarely impacts the stock market alone. Its effects ripple across the economy, causing:

- Job losses as companies cut costs.
- Reduced consumer spending, leading to slower economic growth.

- Strained financial institutions, particularly those heavily exposed to risky assets.

Governments and central banks often step in during crashes, using tools like interest rate cuts, quantitative easing, or bailouts to stabilize markets.

How Fear and Panic Exacerbate Downturns

The stock market is not just a numbers game; it's also deeply influenced by human emotions. Among these, fear and panic stand out as the most destructive forces during market downturns. When fear takes over, rational decision-making often goes out the window, leading to a cycle of self-reinforcing losses. This chapter delves into how fear and panic spread during a downturn and amplify its effects, transforming a manageable correction into a catastrophic crash.

The Psychology of Fear in Financial Markets

Fear is a primal emotion that has evolved to protect us from threats. In financial markets, however, this instinct can backfire. When investors perceive a threat to their wealth—be it a plummeting stock price, economic uncertainty, or bad news—they often act irrationally, selling their assets without fully assessing the situation.

This reaction stems from a psychological phenomenon known as **loss aversion**—the tendency for people to fear losses more than they value gains. Studies have shown that the pain of losing $100 is roughly twice as intense as the pleasure of gaining the same amount. This bias causes investors to overreact to negative news, even if the long-term fundamentals remain strong.

The Snowball Effect of Panic Selling

1. The Initial Trigger

A downturn often begins with a specific event:

- A poor earnings report from a major company.
- A surprise interest rate hike.
- Political instability or a global crisis.

While these events might not warrant mass panic, they can create uncertainty. For investors already on edge, this uncertainty can act as a trigger, causing them to sell their assets to "cut their losses."

2. Herd Mentality and Fear of Missing Out (FOMO)

Fear is contagious. As more people sell their stocks, prices begin to drop further, confirming the fears of others who were previously hesitant to sell. This phenomenon, known as **herd mentality**, amplifies the downturn.

During bull markets, herd mentality often drives irrational exuberance. During bear markets, it leads to irrational despair. In both cases, investors follow the crowd instead of evaluating their decisions independently.

- **FOMO in Reverse:** Just as the fear of missing out drives people to buy stocks during a rally, the fear of being left holding declining assets drives them to sell during a downturn.

3. Margin Calls and Forced Liquidations

As prices fall, leveraged investors—those who borrowed money to buy stocks—face margin calls, requiring them to sell assets to cover their loans. This forced selling adds fuel to the fire, driving prices lower and causing more margin calls in a vicious cycle.

The Role of Media in Amplifying Panic

The media plays a significant role in shaping investor sentiment. During a downturn, headlines often focus on dramatic losses and worst-case scenarios, which can stoke fear and accelerate selling.

- **Panic-Inducing Language:** Words like "crash," "meltdown," and "freefall" dominate headlines, creating a sense of urgency.
- **Constant Updates:** The 24/7 news cycle ensures that negative stories are repeated endlessly, keeping fear at the forefront of investors' minds.

Social media compounds this effect, as rumors and unverified information spread rapidly, creating an echo chamber of fear and uncertainty.

Emotional Decision-Making: The Enemy of Rational Investing

When fear sets in, investors are more likely to make decisions based on emotion rather than logic. Common emotional responses during a downturn include:

1. **Selling Low:** Investors panic-sell their stocks after significant losses, locking in their losses instead of waiting for a potential recovery.

2. **Avoiding the Market Altogether:** Fear of further losses can cause investors to stay out of the market, missing opportunities to buy undervalued assets.

3. **Overreacting to News:** Investors may sell their holdings based on rumors or minor events that have little long-term impact.

These behaviors not only hurt individual investors but also contribute to the overall volatility of the market.

The Spiral of Fear: A Chain Reaction

Fear-driven selling creates a feedback loop that exacerbates the downturn:

1. **Price Declines:** Initial selling causes stock prices to fall.

2. **Loss Aversion:** Declining prices trigger more selling as investors try to avoid further losses.

3. **Market Volatility:** Increased selling creates wild price swings, deterring long-term investors.

4. **Economic Impact:** As stock prices plummet, businesses face reduced valuations, leading to cutbacks, layoffs, and reduced consumer spending.

5. **Deepened Panic:** Economic downturns feed back into market fears, perpetuating the cycle.

Case Studies: Fear in Action

The 2008 Financial Crisis

The collapse of Lehman Brothers in September 2008 sent shockwaves through the financial system. Investors feared that other major banks would also fail, leading to a massive sell-off. This panic was compounded by the opaque nature of the subprime mortgage crisis, which left investors unsure of where the risks were concentrated.

As a result, the S&P 500 lost over 50% of its value from its 2007 peak to its 2009 trough. While the initial trigger was a genuine financial crisis, the extent of the downturn was amplified by fear and uncertainty.

The COVID-19 Pandemic (2020)

In March 2020, the rapid spread of COVID-19 and the ensuing lockdowns created unprecedented uncertainty. Investors feared a global economic collapse, leading to one of the fastest stock market crashes in history. The S&P 500 fell 34% in just over a month.

While the market eventually recovered, the initial panic selling was driven more by uncertainty and fear of the unknown than by concrete financial data.

How to Combat Fear During Downturns

Investors can take steps to minimize the impact of fear on their decision-making:

1. **Stick to a Plan:** Having a well-thought-out investment strategy can help you stay focused on long-term goals rather than short-term fluctuations.

2. **Diversify:** A diversified portfolio reduces risk, making it easier to weather downturns.

3. **Focus on Fundamentals:** Instead of reacting to market noise, base your decisions on the underlying value of your investments.

4. **Limit Media Consumption:** Reduce exposure to sensationalist headlines that can stoke fear.

5. **Seek Professional Advice:** A financial advisor can provide objective guidance during volatile times.

The Role of Institutional Investors and Algorithmic Trading

The modern stock market is a complex ecosystem, and two of its most influential players are institutional investors and algorithmic trading systems. Institutional investors manage vast sums of money on behalf of organizations, while algorithmic trading relies on advanced technologies to execute trades at lightning speed. Together, they shape market movements, amplify volatility during downturns, and play a critical role in how crashes unfold. This chapter examines their influence, particularly during market downturns and crashes.

Understanding Institutional Investors

Institutional investors are organizations that pool money to invest in securities, real estate, and other assets. They include:

- Mutual funds

- Pension funds
- Hedge funds
- Insurance companies
- Sovereign wealth funds

Because of their size, institutional investors dominate trading volumes and have the power to move markets. Their decisions—whether to buy, sell, or hold—are often based on extensive research and sophisticated analysis. However, during periods of market uncertainty, even these seasoned players can contribute to panic and exacerbate downturns.

How Institutional Investors Influence Downturns

1. **Massive Sell-Offs**
   When institutional investors decide to reduce their exposure to risky assets during a downturn, their large-scale selling can trigger or deepen a market decline. A single decision by a hedge fund or pension fund to liquidate billions of dollars' worth of stocks can cause sharp price drops, spooking other investors.

2. **Herd Behavior**
   Despite their resources and expertise, institutional investors are not immune to herd mentality. During periods of uncertainty, they often mimic each other's strategies, amplifying market movements. If one institution sells, others may follow suit to avoid potential losses, leading to a cascading effect.

3. **Impact on Liquidity**
   Liquidity—the ease with which an asset can be bought or sold—declines sharply during a crash. Institutional

investors withdrawing from markets exacerbate this problem. As buyers disappear and sellers flood the market, prices fall even faster.

4. **Forced Selling**
   Many institutional investors, such as mutual funds, face redemption requests during downturns. When individual investors panic and pull their money out, fund managers are forced to sell assets to meet these redemptions, further driving down prices.

   - **Example: The 2008 Financial Crisis**
     During the crisis, institutional investors played a significant role in the sell-off. Hedge funds faced massive redemptions, while mutual funds sold holdings to meet withdrawal demands. This wave of selling accelerated the market's decline.

The Rise of Algorithmic Trading

Algorithmic trading, or algo trading, involves the use of computer programs to execute trades based on predefined criteria, such as price movements, volume, or timing. It now accounts for a significant portion of trading activity in major markets, often exceeding 70% of total trading volume in the U.S.

Algorithms are designed to react faster than humans, executing trades in milliseconds. While this speed and efficiency can improve market liquidity under normal conditions, it can also create chaos during a downturn.

How Algorithmic Trading Amplifies Downturns

1. **Automated Selling in Declining Markets**
   Many algorithms are programmed to sell when prices fall below certain thresholds. During a downturn, these pre-set triggers can lead to widespread selling, pushing prices lower in a short amount of time.
   - **Example: The 2010 Flash Crash**
     On May 6, 2010, the Dow Jones Industrial Average plunged nearly 1,000 points within minutes. High-frequency trading algorithms, designed to react to price changes, entered a feedback loop, selling as prices fell and exacerbating the decline.

2. **Market Liquidity Drain**
   While algorithms provide liquidity in stable markets, they often withdraw it during periods of extreme volatility. When prices fall rapidly, many algorithms stop trading altogether, leaving the market with fewer buyers and intensifying the downturn.

3. **Amplification of Volatility**
   Algorithms are highly sensitive to short-term price movements. During a downturn, this sensitivity can create rapid price swings, making the market more volatile and deterring long-term investors.

4. **Flash Crashes and Mini-Crashes**
   Algorithmic trading can cause sudden, sharp drops in stock prices, known as flash crashes. These events may last only minutes but can erode investor confidence and contribute to broader market instability.

The Interaction Between Institutional Investors and Algorithms

Institutional investors increasingly rely on algorithmic trading to manage their portfolios, blurring the line between the two. This reliance creates a feedback loop during downturns:

- Institutional selling triggers price declines.
- Algorithms react to these declines by selling further.
- The combination of human and machine-driven selling accelerates the market's fall.

Case Studies: Institutional Investors and Algorithms in Action

1. The 2008 Financial Crisis

During the financial crisis, hedge funds and other institutional investors played a pivotal role in the market downturn. As subprime mortgages collapsed, institutions with large exposures to mortgage-backed securities began liquidating their positions. Algorithms compounded the problem by selling assets as prices fell, creating a spiral of declining valuations.

2. The 2018 Volatility Spike

In February 2018, the stock market experienced a sudden spike in volatility, driven in part by algorithmic trading. Many volatility-linked investment products were liquidated, triggering a sharp sell-off. Institutional investors contributed to the decline by exiting positions tied to volatility indices, demonstrating how human and machine strategies can align to exacerbate market turmoil.

Regulation and Safeguards

The growing influence of institutional investors and algorithmic trading has prompted calls for greater regulation to prevent their destabilizing effects during downturns. Measures include:

1. **Circuit Breakers:** Temporary halts in trading when prices fall too quickly, giving markets time to stabilize.

2. **Limits on High-Frequency Trading:** Some regulators have proposed restrictions on the speed and volume of trades to reduce volatility.

3. **Transparency Requirements:** Increased reporting requirements for institutional investors and algorithmic strategies to improve market oversight.

Mitigating the Risks

Investors can protect themselves from the volatility caused by institutional and algorithmic trading by:

1. **Focusing on Fundamentals:** Avoid being swayed by short-term price movements driven by institutional or algorithmic activity.

2. **Diversifying Investments:** Spread your portfolio across asset classes to reduce exposure to sudden market swings.

3. **Staying Informed:** Understanding how institutional investors and algorithms operate can help you anticipate potential risks.

Conclusion

Institutional investors and algorithmic trading are integral to the modern stock market, driving both efficiency and volatility. While they bring advantages such as improved liquidity and faster trade execution, their actions during downturns can amplify market declines. Understanding their role in market dynamics is essential for navigating the complexities of today's financial landscape. By staying informed and maintaining a long-term perspective, individual investors can avoid being swept up in the turbulence caused by these powerful market forces.

CHAPTER 2

COMMON MISTAKES INVESTORS MAKE DURING A CRASH

Selling in Panic

Stock market crashes are a test of an investor's mindset, discipline, and strategy. Unfortunately, many fail this test, often because of fear and panic. The most common mistake during such tumultuous times is selling in panic. While this reaction may feel instinctive, it often leads to regret and significant financial loss. In this chapter, we will explore why investors sell in panic, the consequences of doing so, and how to develop strategies to avoid this costly mistake.

The Psychology Behind Panic Selling

When markets crash, fear takes over. Watching the value of one's portfolio plummet can trigger emotional distress, leading to irrational decision-making. Behavioral economics defines this as *loss aversion*—the fear of losing money is far more potent than the joy of gaining it.

The news media compounds this fear by sensationalizing market downturns with phrases like "historic collapse" or "market freefall." When everyone else seems to be selling, it creates a *herd mentality*, where individual investors feel pressured to follow suit to avoid perceived greater losses. This psychological cocktail of fear, herd behavior, and loss aversion creates a perfect storm for panic selling.

The Consequences of Selling in Panic

Selling during a crash locks in losses. Historically, stock market recoveries have shown that downturns are temporary. By selling, investors lose the opportunity to participate in the eventual rebound. Let's consider two examples:

1. **The 2008 Financial Crisis**: During the global financial meltdown, major indices like the S&P 500 lost over 50% of their value. Many investors panicked and sold their holdings near the bottom, only to see markets recover and grow to all-time highs within a few years. Those who held on reaped the benefits of the recovery, while panic sellers crystallized their losses.

2. **The COVID-19 Crash in 2020**: Markets dropped over 30% in March 2020 as fear of the pandemic spread. However, within months, a robust recovery occurred, with the Nasdaq and S&P 500 reaching record highs by the end of the year. Investors who sold in March not only missed the

recovery but also struggled to reinvest during the rebound.

Why Selling in Panic Feels Justified

Investors often rationalize their panic selling by convincing themselves that staying in the market will result in total financial ruin. However, this logic is rarely sound. Here's why selling in panic often feels "right" but isn't:

1. **Fear of the Unknown**: The future during a crash feels unpredictable, making investors believe that "getting out now" is the safest option.

2. **Short-Term Focus**: Crashes can make long-term investors shift to a short-term perspective, prioritizing immediate damage control over long-term growth.

3. **Misperceived Control**: Selling gives investors a sense of taking action, even if it's detrimental. This illusion of control provides temporary emotional relief but often leads to regret.

Strategies to Avoid Panic Selling

1. **Understand Market Cycles**: Markets operate in cycles of booms and busts. History has shown that every downturn is followed by an upturn. Educating yourself about these cycles can help build confidence to weather the storm.

2. **Have a Long-Term Perspective**: Remind yourself of your financial goals and why you invested in the first place. A well-diversified portfolio designed for long-term growth can endure short-term fluctuations.

3. **Automate Decisions with Stop-Loss Orders**: Setting stop-loss limits can help you sell only when a stock falls to a pre-defined level, reducing emotional decision-making.

4. **Keep a Cash Reserve**: Having a cash reserve ensures that you won't need to sell investments to cover living expenses during a downturn, giving you the flexibility to hold your assets until the market recovers.

5. **Turn Down the Noise**: Avoid over-consuming news and media during crashes. Sensational headlines are designed to grab attention, not to provide rational investment advice.

Case Study: A Tale of Two Investors

Consider two fictional investors, Raj and Meera, during a major market crash:

- **Raj**: Overcome by fear, Raj sold his entire portfolio when the market dropped by 30%. By the time he felt confident enough to reinvest, the market had already rebounded by 40%, and he missed the recovery gains.

- **Meera**: Despite her fears, Meera stayed invested, focusing on the fact that her portfolio was diversified and aligned with her long-term goals. She even bought more shares at discounted prices during the crash.

Over the next three years, her portfolio not only recovered but also grew significantly.

This simple comparison illustrates the power of staying invested and avoiding panic.

The Path Forward: Building Emotional Resilience

Successful investing is as much about controlling emotions as it is about understanding markets. Here are some ways to cultivate emotional resilience:

1. **Practice Mindfulness**: Learn to recognize when emotions like fear are driving your decisions. Taking a step back to evaluate the situation logically can prevent rash actions.
2. **Seek Professional Advice**: If you're uncertain, consulting a financial advisor can provide clarity and help you stick to your investment plan.
3. **Develop a Written Investment Plan**: A well-crafted plan that includes your goals, risk tolerance, and strategies for downturns can serve as a guide during crises, reducing the urge to act impulsively.

Checking Portfolios Excessively and Making Impulsive Decisions

In the age of constant connectivity, technology has made it easier than ever to monitor investments. While keeping tabs on your portfolio is a good practice, excessive checking during a market downturn can lead to emotional decision-making, often to the investor's detriment. This chapter explores why checking portfolios too frequently can be harmful, the psychological effects of doing so, and strategies to maintain discipline.

The Perils of Over-Monitoring

When markets crash, watching the value of your portfolio decline can feel like witnessing a train wreck in slow motion. Many investors, hoping for a sense of control, start checking their accounts multiple times a day. Unfortunately, this behavior often intensifies anxiety rather than alleviating it.

1. **Magnifying Short-Term Losses**: Markets are inherently volatile in the short term, especially during crashes. Frequent monitoring makes these fluctuations appear larger and more alarming than they truly are, leading to unnecessary stress.

2. **Increased Likelihood of Impulsive Actions**: Watching your investments drop by significant percentages day after day can create an urge to "do something." This sense of urgency often results in selling at a loss or making rash trades without a clear strategy.

3. **Emotional Roller Coaster**: Over-monitoring ties your emotions to the market's performance. Each small uptick or downtick becomes a reason for elation or despair, making it harder to stick to long-term plans.

Impulsive Decisions: The Silent Portfolio Killer

Impulsive decisions, such as selling during a downturn or hastily buying into "safe" investments, are often made in reaction to short-term market movements. These decisions typically backfire for the following reasons:

1. **Locking in Losses**: By selling during a crash, investors convert paper losses into real ones. The market's inevitable recovery then happens without them.

2. **Market Timing Fallacy**: Impulsive decisions are often based on the belief that an investor can "time" the market, but studies have shown that even seasoned professionals struggle to consistently predict market movements.

3. **Shift in Strategy**: Emotional decisions often deviate from an investor's original plan, undermining the disciplined approach necessary for long-term success.

Why Investors Check Portfolios Excessively

1. **Availability of Technology**: With smartphones and trading apps, portfolio updates are just a click away. Instant access makes it tempting to check constantly, especially during volatile periods.

2. **Fear of Missing Out (FOMO)**: Investors may feel the need to monitor their accounts obsessively to avoid missing opportunities or to mitigate losses.

3. **Psychological Need for Control**: Checking portfolios frequently gives the illusion of

control over uncontrollable market forces, offering a false sense of security.

How to Avoid Over-Monitoring and Impulsivity

1. **Set a Schedule for Portfolio Reviews**: Limit yourself to checking your portfolio at predetermined intervals—monthly, quarterly, or even annually. This reduces emotional responses to short-term market swings.

2. **Focus on Fundamentals, Not Fluctuations**: Remind yourself that the true value of your investments lies in their long-term potential, not their day-to-day price movements.

3. **Turn Off Notifications**: Disable alerts from trading apps and financial news platforms during volatile periods to avoid being tempted by market noise.

4. **Adopt a "Set and Forget" Mindset**: Trust your investment strategy and allow it to work over time. If your portfolio is well-diversified and aligned with your goals, there's no need for constant monitoring.

Following the Crowd or "Herd Mentality"

During market crashes, one of the most common pitfalls investors face is succumbing to the herd mentality. When panic spreads, it's easy to follow what others are doing, assuming the majority must be right. Unfortunately, this behavior often leads to poor decisions and missed opportunities. In this chapter, we'll dissect the dangers of herd mentality and offer strategies to avoid being swept away by the crowd.

The Dynamics of Herd Mentality

Herd mentality is the tendency to mimic the actions of a larger group, often driven by fear or greed. This behavior is deeply rooted in human psychology:

1. **Safety in Numbers**: People often equate following the crowd with safety, believing that if everyone else is selling or buying, it must be the correct move.

2. **Fear of Missing Out (FOMO)**: When others seem to be capitalizing on an opportunity—or avoiding a perceived threat—it creates an overwhelming desire to join in, even without proper analysis.

3. **Media Amplification**: Sensationalized headlines and viral social media posts can intensify herd behavior by portraying market trends as definitive and urgent.

Consequences of Following the Herd

1. **Buying High, Selling Low**: Herd behavior often results in investors buying at inflated prices during bubbles or selling at rock-bottom prices during crashes, the exact opposite of sound investment practices.

2. **Missing Unique Opportunities**: By blindly following the crowd, investors ignore undervalued assets or contrarian strategies that could lead to significant gains.

3. **Reinforcing Negative Cycles**: Herd mentality can exacerbate market volatility, as widespread panic selling leads to further declines, while overenthusiastic buying creates unsustainable bubbles.

Real-World Examples of Herd Mentality

1. **The Dot-Com Bubble**: In the late 1990s, investors poured money into tech stocks without fully understanding the companies' business models. The bubble burst in 2000, wiping out billions of dollars as investors scrambled to sell, all because "everyone else was doing it."

2. **The Bitcoin Frenzy of 2017**: As Bitcoin's price skyrocketed, millions of investors jumped in, fearing they'd miss out on unprecedented profits. When the market corrected, latecomers suffered massive losses.

How to Resist the Herd Mentality

1. **Develop Independent Thinking**: Focus on your unique financial goals and strategies rather than what others are doing. A well-thought-out plan can help you stay grounded.

2. **Conduct Thorough Research**: Before making any investment decisions, ensure they are based on sound analysis rather than popular sentiment.

3. **Value Contrarian Thinking**: Some of the most successful investors, like Warren Buffett, have built their wealth by going against the crowd. Buffett's famous advice, "Be fearful when others are greedy, and greedy when others are fearful," underscores the importance of contrarian investing.

4. **Ignore Short-Term Noise**: Herd mentality thrives on short-term market events. By focusing on long-term trends, you can avoid being swayed by temporary hysteria.

Over-Leveraging or Holding Non-Diversified Portfolios

Investing is a powerful tool for wealth creation, but it comes with risks that can magnify during market crashes. Two common mistakes that significantly increase vulnerability during a downturn are **over-leveraging** and **holding non-diversified portfolios**. In this chapter, we'll explore what these mistakes entail, why they are dangerous, and how investors can avoid them to safeguard their financial health.

What is Over-Leveraging?

Over-leveraging occurs when an investor borrows money to increase their investment exposure, often through margin loans or other forms of debt. While leverage can amplify returns in a rising market, it also magnifies losses during a downturn.

For example, if you invest $10,000 of your own money and borrow an additional $10,000 to purchase stocks, you now control $20,000 worth of assets. If the market rises by 10%, you gain $2,000—a 20% return on your initial $10,000. However, if the market falls by 10%, your $20,000 investment shrinks to $18,000, and after repaying the $10,000 loan, you're left with just $8,000—a 20% loss on your capital.

In a crash, leveraged investors can face **margin calls**—demands from lenders to repay or add funds to their accounts. If they fail to meet these demands, their positions may be liquidated at a loss, compounding the damage.

The Dangers of Over-Leveraging

1. **Magnified Losses**:
   Leverage doesn't just amplify gains; it amplifies losses, making it far more difficult to recover from a downturn.

2. **Forced Liquidations**:
   A margin call during a crash often forces investors to sell assets at depressed prices, locking in losses and eliminating the chance of recovery.

3. **Emotional Stress**:
   The financial pressure of repaying loans in a declining market creates emotional distress, often leading to rash decisions and financial instability.

What is a Non-Diversified Portfolio?

A non-diversified portfolio is heavily concentrated in one or a few investments, such as a single stock, sector, or asset class. While concentrated portfolios can deliver outsized returns during favorable conditions, they expose investors to significant risks during downturns.

For instance, an investor who puts all their money into technology stocks might see rapid growth during a tech boom. However, if the tech sector crashes, their entire portfolio could be wiped out. Diversification spreads risk across different investments, reducing the impact of any single asset's poor performance.

The Risks of Non-Diversification

1. **Sector-Specific Risks**: Industries are often impacted by unique factors. For example, energy stocks may suffer during periods of low oil prices, while tech stocks may crash when interest rates rise. A non-diversified portfolio tied to one sector is highly vulnerable to these risks.

2. **Overdependence on a Single Asset**: Relying on one stock or asset class increases the likelihood of catastrophic loss if that investment underperforms or collapses.

3. **Limited Recovery Options**: Diversified portfolios often have some assets that perform well even during downturns, providing a cushion for recovery. A non-diversified portfolio lacks this safety net.

Historical Examples of Over-Leveraging and Non-Diversification

1. **The Great Depression (1929)**: Many investors in the 1920s bought stocks on margin. When the market crashed, margin calls forced widespread liquidations, worsening the downturn and leading to financial ruin for millions.

2. **The Dot-Com Bubble (2000)**: During the tech boom, many investors concentrated their portfolios in internet stocks. When the bubble burst, companies with high valuations but no profits collapsed, erasing fortunes for non-diversified investors.

3. **The 2008 Financial Crisis**: Real estate investors who over-leveraged through subprime mortgages faced massive losses when housing prices fell. Similarly, portfolios heavily concentrated in financial stocks took years to recover.

Strategies to Avoid Over-Leveraging

1. **Understand the Risks of Debt**: Borrowing to invest should only be done with a clear understanding of the risks and potential consequences.

2. **Use Leverage Sparingly**: Limit leverage to a small portion of your portfolio and ensure you can meet margin calls without selling assets at a loss.

3. **Maintain a Safety Cushion**: Always have cash or liquid assets available to weather a downturn without relying on credit.

4. **Focus on Long-Term Growth**: Avoid the temptation to use leverage for short-term gains, as the risks often outweigh the rewards.

Strategies for Diversifying Your Portfolio

1. **Invest Across Asset Classes**: Include stocks, bonds, real estate, and other assets in your portfolio. Each asset class responds differently to market conditions, reducing overall risk.

2. **Diversify by Geography**: Investing in international markets can protect against country-specific economic downturns.

3. **Include Defensive Assets**: Defensive investments like gold or utility stocks tend to perform well during market crashes, providing stability to your portfolio.

4. **Use Index Funds or ETFs**: These investment vehicles provide instant diversification across a broad range of assets, making them ideal for risk management.

5. **Rebalance Regularly**: Periodically review and adjust your portfolio to ensure it remains diversified and aligned with your risk tolerance.

Balancing Risk and Reward

Over-leveraging and non-diversification stem from the same desire: to maximize returns. While this ambition is natural, it must be balanced with risk management. Successful investing isn't about chasing the highest possible returns—it's about achieving steady, sustainable growth while protecting your capital.

Conclusion

The twin mistakes of over-leveraging and holding non-diversified portfolios can turn market crashes from temporary setbacks into permanent financial disasters. By avoiding excessive debt and spreading your investments across diverse assets, you can weather downturns with confidence and position yourself for long-term success. Remember, building wealth is a marathon, not a sprint, and the key is to stay disciplined and resilient, even during turbulent times.

CHAPTER 3

THE PSYCHOLOGY OF A CRASH

Financial markets operate not just on numbers and valuations but on the emotions and psychology of the investors participating in them. A stock market crash, more than any other event, lays bare the intricate interplay of fear, loss aversion, and cognitive biases that drive decision-making. Understanding these psychological forces is critical for anyone aiming to navigate a crash effectively.

The Role of Fear in a Crash

Fear is a natural response to uncertainty, and in the context of a stock market crash, it manifests as panic selling. When markets begin to plummet, the instinctive reaction of many investors is to sell their assets in an attempt to "cut their losses." This behavior is not necessarily rational but rather a survival mechanism. However, in financial markets, giving in to fear often exacerbates losses.

Fear amplifies during a crash due to *herd mentality*. When investors see others selling, they assume these actions are based on knowledge they lack. This prompts them to follow suit, creating a self-fulfilling prophecy where prices drop further as more people sell. Understanding this dynamic can help you pause, evaluate the situation objectively, and avoid impulsive decisions.

Loss Aversion: The Pain of Losing

Loss aversion is one of the most significant biases influencing investor behavior during a crash. First identified by behavioral economists Daniel Kahneman and Amos Tversky, loss aversion suggests that the pain of losing is psychologically more powerful than the pleasure of gaining. In practical terms, a loss of $10 feels more intense than the joy of earning $10.

This bias explains why many investors hold on to losing positions for too long, refusing to sell in hopes that the price will recover. Ironically, the same bias can lead others to sell too soon, fearing further losses. Recognizing loss aversion within yourself allows you to make more balanced decisions, even when the market is volatile.

Cognitive Biases That Shape Reactions

Several cognitive biases come into play during a market crash, compounding the challenges of rational decision-making:

1. Recency Bias

Recency bias is the tendency to place greater weight on recent events than historical data. During a crash, this bias leads investors to believe that falling prices will continue indefinitely. They forget that markets are cyclical and often recover over time. Recognizing recency bias can help you step back and evaluate the market's long-term trends.

2. Confirmation Bias

Investors often seek out information that confirms their fears during a crash, ignoring data that contradicts their beliefs. This confirmation bias can lead to overestimating the severity of the situation. For example, reading only pessimistic news articles reinforces a sense of doom, making it harder to stay objective.

3. Anchoring Bias

Anchoring occurs when investors fixate on a specific price point, such as the all-time high of a stock or portfolio. During a crash, this bias can make it difficult to accept the current market reality, leading to poor decision-making. For instance, an investor might refuse to sell a stock that has fallen significantly, clinging to its peak price as the "true value."

Emotional Cycles in a Crash

Investors often experience a predictable emotional cycle during a market crash:

1. **Denial**
   At the onset of a downturn, many investors dismiss the drop as temporary, convincing themselves that recovery is imminent.

2. **Panic**

   As losses mount, denial gives way to panic. Investors sell their holdings to avoid further losses, often locking in significant financial damage.

3. **Despair**

   After selling at a loss, many investors regret their decisions, feeling helpless and reluctant to re-enter the market.

4. **Hope**

   When the market begins to stabilize, a sense of hope emerges, but fear of being wrong again may prevent action.

Understanding this cycle can help you break free from emotional reactions and adopt a more strategic approach during a crash.

The Importance of Mental Discipline

Navigating a crash requires mental discipline and a clear strategy. Here are some steps to help cultivate this discipline:

- **Develop a Plan in Advance**
  A pre-defined investment plan, including stop-losses and diversification, can prevent panic-driven decisions.

- **Focus on Long-Term Goals**
  Crashes are short-term phenomena. Keeping your long-term investment goals in mind can help you stay calm and avoid impulsive actions.

- **Seek Rational Advice**
  During times of market turmoil, consulting a financial

advisor or relying on well-researched data can provide perspective.

Using Psychology to Your Advantage

While crashes reveal the darker side of investor psychology, they also present opportunities for those who can remain calm. Historically, market downturns have been the best times to buy undervalued assets. By understanding and overcoming fear, loss aversion, and biases, you can turn a crash into a wealth-building opportunity.

The key is to remain analytical when others are emotional. As Warren Buffett famously said, *"Be fearful when others are greedy, and greedy when others are fearful."*

A market crash is as much a test of psychology as it is of financial strategy. By understanding the emotional drivers that lead to poor decisions, you can position yourself to act rationally, seizing opportunities while others are paralyzed by fear.

How to Build Emotional Resilience as an Investor

Investing is as much about managing emotions as it is about analyzing numbers. Markets are unpredictable, and the emotional toll of watching your portfolio rise and fall can be significant. Emotional resilience—the ability to stay composed, make rational decisions, and recover quickly from setbacks—is a vital skill for any investor. Here's how to cultivate it.

Start by understanding your emotional triggers. Every investor has unique fears and biases, whether it's the anxiety of losing money or the regret of missed opportunities. Reflect on your past investment decisions to identify patterns. Did you panic and sell during a downturn? Were you overly optimistic during a bull market? Recognizing these tendencies is the first step toward managing them effectively.

Set clear financial goals that anchor your decisions. When you know why you're investing—whether it's for retirement, buying a home, or building generational wealth—you're less likely to be swayed by short-term market volatility. Your goals provide a sense of purpose and a long-term perspective, helping you stay focused when emotions run high.

Educate yourself about market behavior. Fear often stems from the unknown, and understanding how markets work can reduce uncertainty. Learn about historical trends, cycles, and the common causes of volatility. Realize that market crashes are a natural part of the economic cycle and often present opportunities for long-term investors. This knowledge equips you to react with confidence rather than panic.

Diversification is another powerful tool for emotional resilience. When your portfolio includes a mix of asset classes, industries, and geographies, you're less exposed to the risks of any single investment. Knowing that your wealth isn't tied to one stock or sector can ease anxiety during downturns. Diversification not only protects your portfolio but also gives you the peace of mind to think clearly.

Developing a disciplined investment strategy is crucial. Decide in advance how you'll respond to market changes, such as setting stop-loss limits or rebalancing your portfolio periodically. A well-thought-out strategy reduces the need for impulsive decisions and keeps you grounded during uncertainty. Stick to your plan, even when emotions tempt you to stray.

Practicing mindfulness and stress management can significantly enhance emotional resilience. Techniques like deep breathing, meditation, and journaling can help you stay calm and focused. When the markets are turbulent, take a step back to evaluate your emotions objectively. Avoid checking your portfolio obsessively, as this can amplify stress.

Surround yourself with supportive and knowledgeable individuals. Joining investment groups, consulting financial advisors, or discussing your strategies with trusted peers can provide valuable perspective. Hearing different viewpoints can challenge your biases and help you make more balanced decisions.

Focus on the long term rather than daily fluctuations. Emotional resilience comes from understanding that investing is a marathon, not a sprint. Temporary losses are just that—temporary. By concentrating on your broader financial journey, you can weather the inevitable ups and downs with greater composure.

Learn to embrace setbacks as learning opportunities. Every investor makes mistakes, and these experiences can be valuable lessons. Instead of dwelling on what went wrong, analyze what you could do differently in the future. A growth mindset helps you turn challenges into stepping stones toward becoming a better investor.

Finally, celebrate small victories along the way. Acknowledge your progress, whether it's sticking to your plan during a downturn or achieving a modest financial milestone. Positive reinforcement builds confidence and reinforces the habits that foster resilience.

Building emotional resilience takes time and effort, but it's a skill that will serve you well beyond investing. By staying mindful, prepared, and focused on the bigger picture, you can navigate the markets with steadiness and emerge stronger from every challenge.

CHAPTER 4
HOW TO REACT DURING A CRASH

Economic downturns and market crashes are inevitable cycles in the world of investing. While they often cause panic, fear, and confusion among investors, how you react during a crash can significantly impact your financial future. Instead of succumbing to emotional decisions, it's crucial to approach these situations with a clear plan. This chapter provides practical steps to assess your financial situation and respond effectively during a market crash.

Step 1: Stay Calm and Avoid Emotional Decisions

Market crashes can create a whirlwind of fear, amplified by sensational news headlines and peer anxiety. Your first reaction is critical:

- **Pause before acting:** Avoid making immediate decisions, such as selling off assets, without evaluating the situation.

- **Focus on long-term goals:** Remind yourself of why you invested in the first place. Crashes are often temporary, and markets tend to recover over time.

- **Tune out noise:** Limit exposure to panic-inducing media. Instead, seek reliable sources and consult with a trusted financial advisor if necessary.

Remember, reacting impulsively can lead to locking in losses or missing opportunities for growth.

Step 2: Assess Your Financial Position

Understanding your financial situation during a crash is vital for making informed decisions. Here's how to do it:

1. **Review your portfolio:**
    - Evaluate the performance of your investments.
    - Identify which assets have been most affected and determine if they are fundamentally sound or if their decline reflects deeper issues.

2. **Calculate your cash reserves:**
    - Ensure you have enough liquid funds to cover 6–12 months of living expenses.
    - Avoid selling investments prematurely to meet immediate needs if you have sufficient cash reserves.

3. **List all debts:**
    - Prioritize paying off high-interest debts, as these can strain your finances further during economic downturns.
    - If necessary, contact lenders to discuss temporary relief options.

4. **Evaluate income stability:**
    - Assess whether your income sources are secure. In uncertain times, having a contingency plan can reduce financial stress.

Step 3: Stick to Your Investment Strategy (or Reassess It)

A crash can test your commitment to your investment strategy. Here's how to stay on course or adjust when necessary:

- **Diversification matters:** Ensure your portfolio is well-diversified across asset classes (e.g., stocks, bonds, real estate, and commodities). This minimizes the impact of losses in any single sector.

- **Rebalance your portfolio:** If certain asset classes are disproportionately affected, consider rebalancing to restore your intended allocation.

- **Avoid timing the market:** It's nearly impossible to predict when the market will hit bottom. Instead, focus on steady, disciplined investing, such as dollar-cost averaging.

Step 4: Look for Opportunities

While crashes are challenging, they also present opportunities for savvy investors:

1. **Buy undervalued assets:**
   - During a crash, high-quality assets often become undervalued. Conduct thorough research to identify strong companies with sustainable business models and healthy balance sheets.
   - Avoid speculative investments, even if they appear cheap.

2. **Increase contributions (if possible):**
   - If you have stable finances, consider increasing your investment contributions during a downturn. The assets you purchase at lower prices can yield significant returns when the market recovers.

3. **Focus on dividend-paying stocks:**
   - Companies with a history of consistent dividend payments can provide steady income during volatile times.

Step 5: Learn from the Experience

Market crashes offer valuable lessons that can improve your investment approach:

- **Review past mistakes:** Identify any emotional decisions or overlooked risks during the crash.

- **Strengthen your emergency fund:** A robust cash reserve ensures you're better prepared for future downturns.

- **Refine your strategy:** Evaluate whether your investment plan aligns with your risk tolerance and long-term goals.

Case Study: The 2008 Financial Crisis

During the 2008 crisis, many investors panicked and sold off their assets at a loss. However, those who held onto quality stocks or bought during the downturn reaped significant gains as the market rebounded. For example:

- Investors who purchased shares of companies like Apple or Amazon during the crisis witnessed exponential growth in the following decade.

- Warren Buffett famously said, "Be fearful when others are greedy, and greedy when others are fearful," emphasizing the importance of taking a long-term perspective.

Key Takeaways

Reacting to a crash requires a balance of logic, discipline, and patience. By assessing your financial position, sticking to a strategy, and recognizing opportunities, you can navigate market downturns effectively. Remember, wealth-building is a marathon, not a sprint—crashes are just one chapter in the journey.

The Importance of a Long-Term Perspective

In investing, the road to success is often paved with patience, discipline, and a long-term perspective. While short-term market fluctuations can cause anxiety, adopting a long-term outlook helps you focus on your ultimate goals and avoid being derailed by temporary setbacks. This chapter explores why a long-term perspective is crucial, how it shields you from emotional decision-making, and how it builds sustainable wealth over time.

1. Markets Are Naturally Volatile

Financial markets are inherently unpredictable in the short term. Prices of stocks, bonds, and other investments fluctuate due to a variety of factors, including:

- Economic indicators like inflation and interest rates.
- Global events such as political instability or natural disasters.
- Market sentiment driven by fear and greed.

These fluctuations, however, often have little impact on the fundamental value of strong investments over the long term. For example:

- **The S&P 500** has experienced several corrections and bear markets, yet its average annual return over the past century remains approximately 7–10% after adjusting for inflation.
- Investors who stayed invested through downturns like the dot-com crash or the 2008 financial crisis

eventually saw significant portfolio recovery and growth.

Understanding this pattern helps you see downturns as temporary disruptions rather than permanent losses.

2. The Power of Compounding Over Time

One of the greatest advantages of a long-term perspective is the ability to harness the power of compounding. Compounding occurs when your investments generate earnings, and those earnings are reinvested to generate even more returns.

- **Example:** Suppose you invest $10,000 at a 7% annual return.
    - After 10 years: $19,672.
    - After 20 years: $38,696.
    - After 30 years: $76,123. The longer your money remains invested, the more exponential your growth becomes. This underscores the importance of staying the course and avoiding the temptation to withdraw funds prematurely.

3. Emotional Decisions Can Be Costly

Short-term market movements often lead to emotional reactions, such as fear during downturns or greed during bull markets. These emotions can lead to impulsive decisions, such as:

- **Panic selling:** Locking in losses during a market decline out of fear the market will fall further.

- **Chasing trends:** Buying overhyped stocks at inflated prices during bull markets, only to face losses when prices normalize.

Adopting a long-term mindset helps you detach from these emotional impulses and make decisions based on logic and strategy instead of fear or greed.

4. Long-Term Investing Reduces Risk

While all investments carry some level of risk, the longer you hold onto a diversified portfolio, the more those risks are mitigated. Historically, long-term investors experience fewer losses compared to short-term traders.

- Over a 1-year period, stock market returns can be highly volatile, with gains or losses exceeding 20%.

- Over a 20-year period, the probability of negative returns drops significantly. This reduction in risk over time emphasizes the value of patience and consistency in wealth-building.

5. Wealth-Building Requires Time

Building significant wealth doesn't happen overnight. It requires consistent contributions, disciplined investing, and the patience to let your portfolio grow. Successful long-term investors focus on:

- **Strategic asset allocation:** Investing across different asset classes to balance risk and reward.

- **Reinvesting dividends:** Reinvesting earnings rather than spending them accelerates compounding.

- **Avoiding timing the market:** Studies show that missing just a few of the best-performing market days can significantly reduce overall returns.

By keeping your eyes on your long-term goals, you can avoid distractions and build a solid financial foundation.

6. Historical Case Studies of Long-Term Success

- **Warren Buffett:** Known as the "Oracle of Omaha," Buffett built his fortune by investing in undervalued companies and holding them for decades. His investment in Coca-Cola, made in 1988, continues to pay substantial dividends today.

- **The 2008 Financial Crisis:** Investors who sold their stocks during the crisis often locked in steep losses. Those who held on or invested more during the downturn reaped significant rewards when the market recovered.

These examples highlight how staying invested for the long haul often leads to substantial wealth accumulation.

7. Staying Focused on Your Goals

A long-term perspective helps you align your investments with your personal financial goals, such as:

- **Retirement planning:** Building a portfolio that will sustain you through your golden years requires decades of disciplined investing.

- **Wealth creation for future generations:** By maintaining a long-term outlook, you can create a legacy that benefits your family and ensures financial security for years to come.

- **Major life milestones:** Funding goals like buying a home, starting a business, or paying for education becomes more achievable when you invest with patience.

Practical Tips for Maintaining a Long-Term Perspective

1. **Have a clear investment plan:** Define your goals, risk tolerance, and time horizon. Revisit your plan periodically but avoid making drastic changes due to short-term events.

2. **Diversify your portfolio:** Spreading investments across various assets reduces the impact of market volatility on your overall returns.

3. **Avoid checking your portfolio daily:** Frequent monitoring can increase anxiety and lead to impulsive decisions.

4. **Work with a trusted advisor:** A financial professional can provide guidance, help you stay disciplined, and keep your emotions in check.

Strategies for Portfolio Rebalancing and Damage Control

Market crashes, economic downturns, or periods of high volatility can significantly impact your investment portfolio. While it's easy to react emotionally, taking a strategic and disciplined approach to portfolio rebalancing and damage control can help you weather the storm and emerge in a stronger position. This chapter will explore practical strategies for managing your portfolio during difficult times, focusing on how to rebalance effectively and mitigate damage to your investments.

1. Understanding Portfolio Rebalancing

Portfolio rebalancing is the process of adjusting the allocation of assets in your portfolio to maintain your intended risk profile. Over time, due to market fluctuations, some investments may outperform while others underperform, causing your portfolio to drift away from your desired balance. Rebalancing ensures that your portfolio stays aligned with your goals and risk tolerance.

When to Consider Rebalancing:

- **After significant market movements:** If your portfolio's asset allocation has shifted too far from your target due to market changes, rebalancing may be necessary.

- **On a set schedule:** Many investors choose to rebalance on an annual or semi-annual basis, regardless of market performance.

- **After a major life event:** If you experience changes such as retirement, a large inheritance, or a career shift, you may need to adjust your portfolio's allocation.

2. Key Principles of Rebalancing

Rebalancing is more than just adjusting the proportions of your portfolio. It requires a thoughtful and systematic approach to ensure you're making decisions based on long-term goals and not short-term market conditions.

- **Maintain a long-term focus:** Always keep in mind your long-term objectives. Rebalancing should be guided by your risk tolerance and goals, not by short-term market fluctuations.

- **Sell high, buy low:** Rebalancing often means selling assets that have appreciated and buying those that have underperformed. This can help lock in profits while purchasing undervalued assets at a discount.

- **Minimize transaction costs and taxes:** Be mindful of trading fees and capital gains taxes when rebalancing. Where possible, look for tax-efficient ways to make adjustments, such as using tax-advantaged accounts like IRAs or 401(k)s.

3. Rebalancing Strategies

Several rebalancing strategies can help you manage risk and ensure your portfolio remains on track. The right strategy for you will depend on your specific financial situation and goals.

A. Strategic Rebalancing

- **Predefined target allocation:** The most common approach is setting a specific asset allocation based on your risk tolerance (e.g., 60% stocks, 40% bonds). Over time, as some investments grow faster than others, you'll need to sell a portion of the outperforming assets and buy those that have lagged to maintain this balance.

- **Example:** If stocks outperform and grow to 70% of your portfolio, you would sell some of your stock holdings and reinvest the proceeds into bonds or other underperforming assets to return to the original 60/40 split.

B. Tactical Rebalancing

- **Adapting to market conditions:** Tactical rebalancing is more flexible than strategic rebalancing. It involves making adjustments based on current market conditions or short-term market opportunities. This strategy requires active management and a keen understanding of market trends, but can also yield higher returns when done correctly.

- **Example:** If you anticipate a particular sector or asset class will outperform in the near term, you might temporarily allocate more funds to that area while still maintaining a long-term strategy.

C. Dollar-Cost Averaging (DCA)

- **Gradual rebalancing:** Instead of making large adjustments all at once, dollar-cost averaging spreads the rebalancing process over a period of time, reducing the impact of market fluctuations on the overall portfolio. DCA involves investing a set amount of money at regular intervals (e.g., monthly) to gradually rebalance your portfolio.

- **Example:** Rather than selling 20% of your equities to buy bonds in one go, you might instead sell 5% every quarter, buying bonds with the proceeds, which helps avoid market timing risks.

4. Damage Control During a Market Crash

When markets experience a crash or steep decline, your portfolio can take a significant hit. While it's natural to want to react quickly, panicking often leads to poor decisions. Here are steps to help mitigate damage during a market downturn:

A. Stay Calm and Avoid Panic Selling

- **Emotions drive mistakes:** Selling off assets during a market crash locks in losses and may prevent you from benefiting when the market recovers.

- **Think long-term:** Remind yourself that downturns are often temporary, and markets tend to rebound over time. Review your long-term investment strategy and stay focused on your goals.

B. Reassess Your Risk Tolerance

- **Volatility tolerance:** A crash can test your ability to handle risk. Reevaluate your risk tolerance, especially if you feel uncomfortable with the declines in your portfolio. If necessary, you may need to adjust your portfolio's asset allocation, reducing exposure to higher-risk assets.

- **Example:** If you have a high stock allocation and your risk tolerance has changed due to the crash, you may choose to move a portion of your investments into more stable, conservative assets like bonds or cash.

C. Take Advantage of Market Opportunities

- **Buy undervalued assets:** During a market downturn, quality assets often become undervalued. If you have the financial stability to do so, this can be an excellent time to purchase stocks, bonds, or real estate at discounted prices.

- **Example:** If stocks of high-quality companies like Apple or Amazon fall significantly, but the underlying fundamentals remain solid, this could be a buying opportunity.

D. Use Tax-Loss Harvesting

- **Offset capital gains:** Tax-loss harvesting involves selling investments that have declined in value to offset taxable gains in other areas of your portfolio. This can help reduce your tax liability, even during a market downturn.

- **Example:** If you have other investments that are up in value, you can sell underperforming stocks to realize the losses and use them to offset taxes on your gains.

5. When to Seek Professional Help

While DIY rebalancing and damage control can be effective for many investors, there may be times when it's beneficial to seek the help of a financial advisor:

- **Complex portfolios:** If you have a highly diversified or complex portfolio, such as investments in real estate, commodities, or international stocks, a financial advisor can help ensure your rebalancing strategy aligns with your long-term goals.

- **Tax considerations:** A professional can guide you on tax-efficient rebalancing strategies, such as utilizing tax-advantaged accounts or taking advantage of tax-loss harvesting.

- **Emotional support:** If market downturns are causing emotional stress, a financial advisor can help provide perspective and reassurance, helping you avoid rash decisions based on fear.

6. Final Thoughts

Effective portfolio rebalancing and damage control during a crash are essential skills for any investor. By staying disciplined, focusing on your long-term goals, and utilizing a well-thought-out strategy, you can navigate market volatility and position your portfolio for future growth. Whether you're actively rebalancing, taking advantage of market opportunities, or simply staying the course, the key to success during turbulent times is a steady hand and a focus on the future.

CHAPTER 5

TURNING A CRISIS INTO AN OPPORTUNITY

A stock market crash can be a terrifying event, but for savvy investors, it's a time ripe with potential. While panic often grips the market, pushing prices to irrational lows, these periods also offer the opportunity to acquire valuable assets at discounted prices. The key is to maintain a rational mindset and a long-term perspective, allowing you to spot undervalued stocks and sectors that are likely to rebound and thrive.

When the market plummets, many stocks are dragged down irrespective of their true value. Fear and herd mentality dominate, causing even fundamentally strong companies to see their share prices tumble. This is where opportunity lies. Investors who can look past the chaos and focus on intrinsic value can turn these crises into wealth-building opportunities.

The first step in identifying undervalued stocks is to focus on their fundamentals. Look for companies with a strong balance sheet, low debt levels, and consistent revenue growth. These firms are more likely to weather the storm of a crash and recover swiftly once the market stabilizes. Pay close attention to their price-to-earnings (P/E) ratio and compare it to their historical average or industry peers. If the ratio is significantly lower, it could signal that the stock is undervalued.

Sectors that are temporarily out of favor during a crash can also present lucrative opportunities. For instance, during the COVID-19 market crash, industries such as travel, hospitality, and retail suffered significant losses. However, investors who recognized the eventual recovery of these sectors were able to purchase shares in companies like airlines and hotel chains at a fraction of their pre-crash prices. The key is to determine whether the downturn in a sector is a short-term reaction to external events or a sign of deeper structural issues.

Diversification is another critical strategy when investing during a crash. Instead of betting heavily on one or two stocks, spread your investments across multiple sectors and industries. This approach minimizes risk while still allowing you to benefit from potential recoveries. Exchange-traded funds (ETFs) focused on specific sectors can also be a good option, as they provide broad exposure to a range of companies.

Timing is another essential factor in turning a crisis into an opportunity. While it's impossible to predict the market's bottom, dollar-cost averaging can help you mitigate the risks associated with trying to time your investments. By investing a fixed amount regularly, you can smooth out the effects of market volatility and build your positions gradually.

Finally, remember that patience is crucial. Recoveries from market crashes take time, and attempting to chase quick gains can lead to costly mistakes. Keep your focus on the long-term potential of your investments and resist the urge to react emotionally to short-term fluctuations. Legendary investors like Warren Buffett emphasize the importance of being "fearful when others are greedy and greedy when others are fearful." This mindset can help you make rational decisions when others are succumbing to panic.

By staying disciplined, focusing on fundamentals, and maintaining a diversified approach, you can transform a market crash into a wealth-building opportunity. History has shown that every major downturn is followed by a recovery, and those who remain calm and strategic during the crisis are often the ones who come out ahead.

Dollar-Cost Averaging During Market Lows

Dollar-cost averaging (DCA) is a strategy that can be especially effective during market lows, particularly when fear and uncertainty dominate the investing landscape. It involves investing a fixed amount of money at regular intervals, regardless of market conditions. This method reduces the emotional impact of market volatility and ensures that investors stay disciplined in their approach, buying more shares when prices are low and fewer when prices are high.

The core advantage of dollar-cost averaging is that it helps mitigate the risk of trying to time the market. During periods of market downturns, investors often face the temptation to wait for the perfect moment to buy, hoping for a definitive "bottom" in prices. Unfortunately, timing the market is nearly impossible, even for seasoned investors, and waiting for the ideal entry point can lead to missed opportunities. Dollar-cost averaging removes the need to predict the market's direction, focusing instead on consistent investment over time.

When markets are in a downturn, such as during a crash or significant correction, prices are typically lower than they were in more stable periods. By employing DCA during these times, an investor automatically purchases more shares when prices are down, effectively lowering the average cost of each share over time. This can result in a more favorable long-term cost basis when the market eventually recovers.

For example, consider an investor who decides to invest $1,000 per month into a broad market index fund. During a market low, the share price of the fund might be $100, allowing the investor to buy 10 shares that month. The following month, if the market has bounced back and the share price increases to $110, the investor would only be able to purchase approximately 9.1 shares. Over time, this process ensures that the investor accumulates more shares when prices are depressed, which can lead to higher returns when the market rebounds.

One of the key benefits of dollar-cost averaging is that it helps to remove emotional decision-making from the investing process. It's easy to become caught up in the panic during market lows, wanting to sell investments to avoid further losses, or conversely, trying to time the market by buying at the "bottom." DCA takes the emotion out of this decision-making, as the investor continues to contribute regardless of market conditions.

However, while dollar-cost averaging can be a powerful tool, it's not a foolproof strategy. It's important to keep in mind that the method works best when combined with a solid investment plan, diversified portfolio, and long-term strategy. For instance, DCA works well with stocks, bonds, or ETFs, but it might not be as effective if you're investing in highly speculative assets or individual stocks that are fundamentally weak or at risk of failure.

Moreover, dollar-cost averaging during market lows doesn't guarantee immediate returns, as there may be periods when prices continue to fall after your investment. However, if your investments are in solid, long-term assets with strong growth potential, DCA allows you to take advantage of the eventual market recovery, which historically occurs after downturns.

Another key consideration when using DCA during market lows is the investor's time horizon. If you are investing for long-term goals, such as retirement, DCA allows you to ride out short-term volatility without the stress of daily market fluctuations. This long-term focus is essential, as markets will inevitably recover from downturns, although the timing is unpredictable.

In conclusion, dollar-cost averaging during market lows is an effective strategy for reducing risk, minimizing the impact of market volatility, and capitalizing on opportunities when prices are down. By maintaining a disciplined, regular investment schedule, investors can gradually build their portfolios at lower average prices, ultimately positioning themselves to benefit when the market recovers. Like any investing strategy, DCA requires patience and a commitment to a long-term vision, but it can be an excellent way to weather market storms and turn a crisis into an opportunity.

Learning from Warren Buffett's Approach to Market Downturns

Warren Buffett, one of the most successful investors of all time, has a unique and highly effective approach to market downturns that has helped him amass a fortune over decades. His strategy revolves around discipline, patience, and a deep understanding of market behavior. By learning from Buffett's methods, investors can develop a mindset that allows them to thrive during market downturns and turn potential setbacks into opportunities.

1. Embrace the Long-Term Perspective

One of the key elements of Buffett's approach is his focus on the long term. He has famously said, "Our favorite holding period is forever." While many investors panic during market downturns, fearing that the losses will never recover, Buffett remains unfazed. He understands that the market is cyclical, and downturns are part of the natural ebb and flow of the economy. Buffett views the temporary losses during a crash as opportunities to acquire high-quality assets at discounted prices, rather than as threats to his wealth.

When the market declines, Buffett doesn't rush to make drastic changes to his portfolio. Instead, he continues to focus on companies with strong fundamentals and long-term growth potential. His strategy is to hold investments for the long haul, only selling when he believes the underlying business no longer meets his investment criteria. This approach allows him to ignore short-term market fluctuations and focus on the intrinsic value of his holdings.

2. Be Greedy When Others Are Fearful

Buffett is renowned for his famous quote: "Be fearful when others are greedy and greedy when others are fearful."

During market downturns, fear often drives widespread selling, and many investors panic, dumping their holdings at discounted prices. Buffett sees these times as opportunities to buy solid companies at a bargain.

This strategy is rooted in the idea that many market participants overreact to short-term news, causing temporary dislocations in stock prices. When the market is in a state of fear, solid companies that have strong fundamentals but face temporary challenges can be purchased at attractive prices. Buffett's ability to remain calm and make strategic investments during these times has been a key factor in his success.

3. Stick to What You Know

Buffett's investment philosophy revolves around sticking to what he knows best—businesses with predictable earnings, competitive advantages, and a proven track record of management excellence. During market downturns, many investors may be tempted to diversify into unfamiliar sectors or riskier investments in an attempt to "buy the dip." However, Buffett advises against this approach. He stresses the importance of investing only in businesses and industries you fully understand.

During a market downturn, sticking to what you know provides clarity in uncertain times. Buffett focuses on companies he can easily evaluate based on their fundamentals, whether it's a consumer brand like Coca-Cola or a financial giant like American Express. He knows that these companies will eventually recover from short-term setbacks and continue to thrive in the long run.

4. Maintain Liquidity and Avoid Panic Selling

Warren Buffett often speaks about the importance of maintaining liquidity during times of market turmoil. He has always kept a substantial cash reserve, which allows him to act quickly when opportunities arise. When the market is down, he is able to deploy capital into high-quality companies at a discount, capitalizing on the fear and uncertainty that others may be succumbing to.

On the flip side, Buffett advises against panic selling. When the market is in a downturn, it's tempting to sell investments to minimize losses. However, Buffett's approach is to resist this impulse, as selling in a downturn only locks in losses. Instead, he views downturns as a natural part of the investment process and an opportunity to reassess his holdings without the pressure of immediate market conditions.

5. Focus on Intrinsic Value, Not Market Price

Buffett emphasizes the importance of focusing on intrinsic value rather than short-term market price fluctuations. The market often misprices stocks, particularly during periods of high volatility. Rather than reacting to the daily ups and downs of stock prices, Buffett takes a long-term view and evaluates companies based on their true value—their ability to generate consistent profits over time.

This perspective is crucial during market downturns when prices may not reflect the underlying value of a company. By focusing on intrinsic value, Buffett can ignore temporary price drops that occur during market corrections and downturns, knowing that solid businesses with strong earnings power will eventually recover. He looks for businesses with durable competitive advantages that will continue to generate profits and grow in the long run, regardless of short-term market conditions.

6. Take Advantage of Market Inefficiencies

Buffett has a talent for spotting market inefficiencies, especially during downturns. When fear dominates the market, stock prices can become disconnected from the true value of a company. This provides an opportunity for investors like Buffett to swoop in and buy undervalued stocks. His approach during market downturns often involves analyzing companies with strong fundamentals that are temporarily oversold.

For example, during the 2008 financial crisis, Buffett took advantage of the market's panic by making strategic investments in companies like Goldman Sachs and General Electric. While others were selling in fear, Buffett recognized the underlying value of these companies and was able to acquire stakes at a steep discount. Over time, these investments paid off handsomely as the market recovered.

7. Don't Try to Time the Market

One of Buffett's most important lessons is that it's nearly impossible to time the market successfully. While many investors try to predict the next market downturn or recovery, Buffett focuses on making consistent, long-term investments rather than attempting to time the market's highs and lows.

During a market downturn, trying to predict the bottom can lead to missed opportunities. Buffett, instead, advocates for investing with a long-term horizon, understanding that the market will eventually recover from its temporary setbacks. His belief in the resilience of the economy and the strength of high-quality businesses helps him avoid the temptation of market timing.

8. Take a Contrarian Approach

Buffett is a well-known contrarian investor. When others are running for the exits, he sees opportunity. Market downturns often trigger widespread pessimism and herd mentality, causing stocks to be sold off indiscriminately. Buffett's contrarian approach involves stepping back from the emotional response of the crowd and looking for opportunities where the market is overreacting.

By being willing to go against the crowd, Buffett has been able to pick up undervalued stocks during times when others are fleeing. This approach requires a strong conviction in one's investment strategy and the courage to hold fast when others are panicking. Buffett's success has shown that taking a contrarian stance during downturns, when supported by sound analysis, can lead to outsized returns in the long run.

Conclusion

Warren Buffett's approach to market downturns provides valuable lessons for investors looking to navigate periods of volatility. By focusing on long-term value, maintaining discipline, and taking advantage of market inefficiencies, investors can turn market downturns into opportunities. Buffett's ability to remain calm, patient, and strategic during times of crisis has been a cornerstone of his success. By learning from his methods, investors can adopt a more thoughtful, rational approach to investing, which can help them not only survive market downturns but thrive in the aftermath.

CHAPTER 6

LESSONS FROM HISTORICAL CRASHES

Introduction

The stock market, with all its allure and unpredictability, is a dynamic battlefield where fortunes are made and lost. However, history shows that even during its darkest moments—economic crashes—companies and investors have not only survived but emerged stronger. This chapter delves into key lessons drawn from historical market crashes, showcasing case studies of resilient companies and strategic investors who turned adversity into opportunity.

The Great Depression (1929-1939): Ford Motor Company's Reinvention

The Great Depression was a seismic economic event that wiped out billions of dollars in wealth and pushed countless businesses into bankruptcy. Yet, amidst the turmoil, Ford

Motor Company stood as a beacon of resilience and reinvention.

During the Depression, Henry Ford adopted a counter-cyclical strategy. While competitors were cutting back on production and laying off workers, Ford invested in innovation. He focused on improving assembly line efficiency and lowering production costs. In 1932, amidst the economic downturn, Ford introduced the flathead V8 engine, a revolutionary innovation in the automotive industry.

Lesson: Economic downturns are opportunities to innovate and invest in future growth. Companies that embrace innovation during crises often capture significant market share once recovery begins.

The 1973-1974 Oil Crisis: Warren Buffett's Investment in The Washington Post

The oil embargo of 1973 led to a global economic slowdown and a severe bear market. Amid this crisis, Warren Buffett demonstrated the power of value investing.

Buffett identified *The Washington Post Company* as a deeply undervalued asset during the downturn. While most investors were selling off stocks in panic, Buffett analyzed the company's intrinsic value and purchased a significant stake at a fraction of its worth. Over the years, his investment grew exponentially, delivering outsized returns.

Lesson: Crashes often lead to irrational market behavior. By focusing on fundamentals and intrinsic value, investors can uncover bargains that yield substantial long-term gains.

The Dot-Com Bubble Burst (2000-2002): Amazon's Survival and Growth

The late 1990s saw a surge of speculative investments in technology companies, many of which were overvalued and unsustainable. When the bubble burst, countless dot-com companies collapsed, but Amazon.com emerged stronger.

Amazon's founder, Jeff Bezos, adopted a disciplined approach, focusing on building a sustainable business rather than chasing short-term profits. While the company's stock price plummeted during the crash, Bezos concentrated on improving operational efficiency, expanding product offerings, and nurturing customer loyalty. By the time the market recovered, Amazon was positioned as a leader in e-commerce.

Lesson: Companies that prioritize long-term strategies over short-term gains can weather market crashes and emerge as industry leaders.

The 2008 Financial Crisis: Goldman Sachs' Strategic Adaptation

The 2008 financial crisis, triggered by the collapse of Lehman Brothers and the housing market crash, brought the global financial system to its knees. Many banks and financial institutions faltered, but Goldman Sachs managed to not only survive but thrive.

Goldman Sachs took swift action, securing a $5 billion investment from Warren Buffett's Berkshire Hathaway, which restored market confidence. Simultaneously, the firm restructured its operations, tightened risk management protocols, and diversified its revenue streams. By the time the economy stabilized, Goldman Sachs had strengthened its market position.

Lesson: Proactive measures and strong partnerships can help companies navigate crises and rebuild trust in turbulent times.

The COVID-19 Pandemic Crash (2020): Tesla's Resilience and Growth

The COVID-19 pandemic caused one of the fastest market crashes in history. Amidst widespread uncertainty, Tesla demonstrated remarkable resilience.

While the auto industry faced significant disruptions, Tesla leveraged its direct-to-consumer sales model and continued expanding its global presence. The company also ramped up its focus on renewable energy products, capturing market trends. By the end of 2020, Tesla's stock price soared, making it one of the most valuable companies in the world.

Lesson: Companies aligned with emerging trends and adaptable business models can outperform even during global crises.

Key Takeaways for Investors and Businesses

1. **Invest in Innovation:** Crises often separate companies that stagnate from those that innovate. Businesses that prioritize research, development, and new offerings during downturns position themselves for success in recovery periods.

2. **Focus on Fundamentals:** Investors who assess companies based on intrinsic value and long-term

growth potential can identify lucrative opportunities during market sell-offs.

3. **Adaptability is Crucial:** Companies that adapt quickly to changing circumstances and emerging trends often outperform their competitors.

4. **Leverage Partnerships:** Strategic partnerships, like Goldman Sachs securing funding from Warren Buffett, can provide the resources and confidence needed to navigate tough times.

5. **Remain Patient and Disciplined:** History rewards those who remain calm and disciplined during market crashes. Emotional decisions often lead to missed opportunities or avoidable losses.

Patterns and Insights from Past Recoveries

Introduction

Market crashes may bring despair, but history demonstrates that recoveries are as inevitable as downturns. Each recovery carries valuable lessons, highlighting patterns and strategies that investors and businesses can use to prepare for future rebounds. This chapter explores the recurring trends seen in past recoveries and provides actionable insights for navigating post-crisis markets effectively.

1. The Power of Patience: Markets Always Recover Over Time

One of the most consistent patterns in history is that markets recover. The timeline varies—sometimes months, other times years—but economic growth eventually resumes. For example:

- After the Great Depression, the Dow Jones Industrial Average (DJIA) took nearly 25 years to reach its pre-crash highs, but those who remained invested saw their portfolios grow significantly.

- Following the 2008 financial crisis, the S&P 500 recovered its losses within five years, reaching new record highs by 2013.

Insight: Recovery is often a game of patience. Investors who avoid panic selling during downturns typically benefit the most when the market rebounds.

2. Sectoral Shifts: Not All Industries Recover Equally

Recoveries often see certain industries and sectors outpace others. These shifts are shaped by the nature of the crash and emerging trends. For instance:

- After the dot-com bubble burst, the technology sector underwent significant consolidation. Survivors like Amazon and eBay emerged as leaders, while weaker companies vanished.

- Following the 2008 crisis, the financial sector recovered slowly, while technology and healthcare led the way, fueled by innovation and demographic changes.

- In the COVID-19 recovery, tech companies focusing on remote work, e-commerce, and cloud services saw explosive growth, whereas traditional retail and travel industries faced prolonged challenges.

Insight: Understanding sectoral dynamics is crucial during recoveries. Investors who align with emerging trends often outperform the market.

3. Government Intervention: A Catalyst for Recovery

Governments and central banks play a pivotal role in stabilizing economies after crashes. Key examples include:

- **The New Deal (1933):** Following the Great Depression, the U.S. government introduced massive public works programs and financial reforms, which laid the foundation for recovery.

- **Quantitative Easing (2008):** Central banks injected liquidity into the financial system, lowering interest rates and encouraging borrowing and investment.

- **Stimulus Packages (2020):** During the COVID-19 pandemic, unprecedented fiscal stimulus measures, including direct payments and business loans, helped support consumer spending and economic activity.

Insight: Monitoring government policies during a recovery provides critical clues about which sectors and markets may rebound the fastest.

4. The Role of Consumer Confidence in Driving Recovery

Recoveries often hinge on the restoration of consumer and investor confidence. As optimism returns, spending and investment pick up, accelerating economic growth.

- In the aftermath of the 2008 financial crisis, consumer confidence steadily improved, driving a resurgence in housing, retail, and automotive sectors.

- During the COVID-19 recovery, vaccine rollouts boosted confidence, leading to a sharp rebound in travel and hospitality industries.

Insight: Gauging consumer sentiment can help investors identify inflection points in the recovery cycle. Leading indicators, such as the Consumer Confidence Index, are valuable tools.

5. The "First Movers" Advantage: Early Investors Reap the Greatest Rewards

Investors and companies that act decisively during the early stages of recovery often outperform those who wait. Examples include:

- In the early 1980s, Warren Buffett capitalized on undervalued stocks during the recovery from stagflation, leading to massive returns for Berkshire Hathaway.

- Tesla expanded aggressively in the years following the 2008 crash, positioning itself as a dominant player in the electric vehicle market.

Insight: While timing the market is challenging, early investments in strong, undervalued assets during recovery phases typically yield significant gains.

6. Innovation as a Driving Force

Crises often accelerate innovation, creating opportunities for businesses that adapt quickly. Historical recoveries show that companies embracing change often emerge as leaders.

- During the Great Depression, General Electric invested in new technologies, including fluorescent lighting, positioning itself for growth in the post-recovery era.

- The COVID-19 recovery saw the rapid adoption of digital tools, benefiting companies like Zoom, Shopify, and Peloton.

Insight: Businesses and investors who identify and align with innovative trends early in a recovery can achieve outsized success.

7. The Importance of Diversification

While some sectors recover faster than others, a diversified portfolio cushions against uncertainty and captures broad market growth.

- After the 2000 dot-com crash, investors with exposure to sectors beyond technology, such as healthcare and consumer goods, experienced less severe losses and benefited from a balanced recovery.

- During the COVID-19 recovery, diversification across international markets helped investors capitalize on global rebounds.

Insight: Diversification remains one of the most reliable strategies for navigating recoveries, minimizing risks while maximizing potential gains.

Key Takeaways for Investors and Businesses

1. **Stay Invested:** Selling during downturns often locks in losses. Maintaining a long-term perspective is crucial for benefiting from recoveries.

2. **Follow the Money:** Monitor government policies and fiscal measures to identify sectors poised for growth.

3. **Be Agile:** Recovery phases reward adaptability. Both businesses and investors should remain flexible and ready to pivot as opportunities emerge.

4. **Focus on Fundamentals:** Post-crash recoveries often favor companies with strong balance sheets, competitive advantages, and growth potential.

5. **Embrace Trends:** Crises reshape industries. Investing in emerging trends like green energy, AI, or healthcare innovation can yield significant rewards.

CHAPTER 7

BUILDING A CRASH-RESILIENT PORTFOLIO

In the world of investing, the only certainty is uncertainty. Markets rise, fall, and sometimes crash, leaving even the savviest investors scrambling. While no one can predict the exact timing or magnitude of a market crash, building a resilient portfolio can minimize losses and position you to recover quickly—and even thrive—in the aftermath. This chapter delves into two essential strategies: **diversification** and **asset allocation**, both of which are cornerstones of a crash-resilient portfolio.

The Importance of Diversification

Diversification is often referred to as the "only free lunch" in investing. It reduces the risk of significant losses by spreading your investments across various asset classes, sectors, geographies, and financial instruments. The idea is simple: when one part of your portfolio is underperforming, another might be performing well, offsetting potential losses.

1. **Diversifying Across Asset Classes**

The first layer of diversification involves spreading investments across asset classes like stocks, bonds, real estate, commodities, and cash. Each asset class reacts differently to economic events. For instance:

- **Stocks** typically offer higher returns over the long term but are more volatile during market crashes.
- **Bonds** provide stability and act as a counterbalance to equities, often performing better in downturns.
- **Real Estate** can offer steady income through rental yields and act as a hedge against inflation.
- **Commodities** like gold tend to be safe havens during periods of economic uncertainty.
- **Cash** or cash-equivalents provide liquidity and the flexibility to take advantage of market opportunities during crashes.

By allocating funds across these categories, you can reduce the overall volatility of your portfolio.

2. **Diversifying Within Asset Classes**

Once you've chosen your asset classes, the next step is diversification within each class. For stocks, this means investing in companies across various sectors (e.g., technology, healthcare, energy, and consumer goods) and geographies (e.g., domestic and international markets). Similarly, for bonds, you might consider government bonds, corporate bonds, and high-yield bonds to balance risk and reward.

3. The Role of ETFs and Mutual Funds

Exchange-Traded Funds (ETFs) and mutual funds offer built-in diversification by pooling funds to invest in a basket of assets. For instance, an S&P 500 index fund provides exposure to 500 of the largest U.S. companies, reducing the impact of a single stock's poor performance.

The Power of Asset Allocation

While diversification involves spreading your investments, **asset allocation** determines the proportion of your portfolio invested in each asset class. This strategy plays a crucial role in achieving a balance between risk and return, particularly during market crashes.

1. Understanding Risk Tolerance

Asset allocation starts with assessing your risk tolerance. Ask yourself:

- How much loss can I handle without panicking?
- What are my financial goals and timelines?

For instance, a young investor saving for retirement might allocate more to stocks due to their growth potential, while a retiree might prioritize bonds for stability and income.

2. Strategic vs. Tactical Allocation

- **Strategic Asset Allocation** is a long-term approach where you set target allocations and periodically rebalance your portfolio to maintain them.
- **Tactical Asset Allocation** involves making short-term adjustments based on market conditions. For example,

during signs of an impending crash, you might temporarily increase your allocation to cash or bonds.

3. The 60/40 Rule—And Why It's Changing

Traditionally, a 60/40 portfolio (60% stocks, 40% bonds) has been a popular allocation strategy. However, with changing market dynamics, investors are exploring alternative allocations, such as adding real estate or commodities to the mix for greater resilience.

Rebalancing: Staying on Course

Market crashes can disrupt your carefully planned asset allocation. For example, a sharp decline in stock prices might shift your portfolio to 40% stocks and 60% bonds, making it more conservative than intended.

Rebalancing involves buying or selling assets to restore your original allocation. This disciplined approach ensures you "buy low and sell high," a fundamental principle of investing.

Stress-Testing Your Portfolio

Before the next market crash hits, it's wise to stress-test your portfolio. Simulate different scenarios—such as a 30% drop in equities or rising interest rates—and evaluate how your portfolio would perform. Tools like Monte Carlo simulations can provide valuable insights into potential outcomes and help you make adjustments proactively.

Case Study: The Resilient Portfolio in Action

Consider two investors:

- **Investor A** holds a portfolio concentrated in technology stocks. During the 2000 dot-com bubble burst, they lost nearly 80% of their portfolio's value.

- **Investor B** has a diversified portfolio with 50% stocks, 30% bonds, 10% real estate, and 10% commodities. While they experienced losses in stocks, gains in bonds and commodities cushioned the blow, and their overall portfolio declined by only 15%.

Investor B recovered faster, demonstrating the power of diversification and asset allocation.

Building Your Crash-Resilient Portfolio: A Checklist

1. **Diversify broadly** across asset classes, sectors, and geographies.
2. **Tailor your asset allocation** to your risk tolerance and goals.
3. **Use low-cost ETFs or mutual funds** for easy diversification.
4. **Periodically rebalance** to maintain your target allocation.
5. **Stress-test your portfolio** for potential crashes.
6. **Keep a cash reserve** to seize opportunities during downturns.

Building a crash-resilient portfolio is not about avoiding losses entirely—that's impossible. Instead, it's about minimizing the damage and positioning yourself to recover and grow in the aftermath. By combining diversification and thoughtful asset allocation, you can weather any storm the market throws your way and emerge stronger on the other side.

Hedging Strategies Using Options, Gold, or Bonds

When market volatility spikes or a crash looms on the horizon, investors seek ways to hedge their portfolios. Hedging involves using financial instruments or assets to offset potential losses. While no hedge can eliminate all risks, a well-executed strategy can provide a safety net to protect your wealth. This chapter explores three popular hedging tools: **options**, **gold**, and **bonds**, and how to effectively use them to safeguard your portfolio.

Hedging with Options

Options are one of the most powerful tools for hedging. They give investors the right, but not the obligation, to buy or sell an asset at a specified price by a certain date. This flexibility makes them ideal for protecting against downside risks.

1. Put Options

A put option gives you the right to sell an asset at a specific price, known as the **strike price**, regardless of its market value.

- **How it works**: If you own shares of a stock and fear a price drop, you can buy a put option as insurance. If the stock's price falls below the strike price, the put option gains value, offsetting losses in the stock.

- **Example**: Suppose you own 100 shares of a company trading at $50 per share. You buy a put option with a $50 strike price for $2 per share. If the stock price drops to $40, you can sell your shares at $50, minimizing your losses.

2. Covered Calls

A covered call involves selling a call option on a stock you already own. While this strategy is often used for generating income, it also provides a partial hedge by offsetting some downside risks.

- **How it works**: By selling a call, you receive a premium, which cushions minor losses if the stock price drops. However, this strategy limits your upside potential.

3. Protective Collars

A collar strategy combines a long put and a short call.

- **How it works**: You buy a put to protect against downside risk and sell a call to generate income, which partially offsets the cost of the put. This creates a range within which your portfolio's value is relatively stable.

4. Index Options

Investors can also hedge broader market exposure using index options, such as those tied to the S&P 500 or Nasdaq. Buying puts on an index ETF can protect against market-wide declines.

Hedging with Gold

Gold has been a trusted store of value for centuries and is often referred to as a "safe haven" asset. During periods of economic uncertainty or market crashes, gold prices typically rise as investors flock to its perceived stability.

1. Why Gold Works as a Hedge

- **Inverse Relationship with the Dollar**: Gold often moves inversely to the U.S. dollar. When the dollar weakens, gold prices tend to rise.
- **Inflation Hedge**: Gold maintains its value during periods of inflation, preserving purchasing power.
- **Crisis Protection**: During geopolitical tensions or financial crises, gold's value usually increases as a flight-to-safety asset.

2. Ways to Invest in Gold

- **Physical Gold**: Buying gold bars or coins offers direct ownership. While secure, it requires storage and insurance.
- **Gold ETFs**: Exchange-traded funds like SPDR Gold Shares (GLD) provide exposure to gold prices without the need for physical storage.
- **Gold Mining Stocks**: Investing in gold miners can provide leveraged exposure to gold prices, although these stocks carry their own risks.
- **Gold Futures**: Futures contracts allow you to speculate on gold prices. However, they are more complex and suitable for experienced investors.

3. Allocating Gold in Your Portfolio

Experts often recommend allocating 5-10% of your portfolio to gold as a hedge against market downturns. This proportion ensures stability without sacrificing too much growth potential.

Hedging with Bonds

Bonds are a cornerstone of portfolio hedging due to their stability and predictable income. During market crashes, investors typically shift from riskier assets (like stocks) to safer ones (like bonds), driving up bond prices.

1. Why Bonds Work as a Hedge

- **Lower Volatility**: Bonds are less volatile than stocks, providing a steady income stream.
- **Negative Correlation**: High-quality bonds, especially U.S. Treasury bonds, often move inversely to stocks during economic downturns.
- **Income Generation**: Bonds provide regular interest payments, which can offset portfolio losses.

2. Types of Bonds for Hedging

- **Treasury Bonds**: U.S. Treasury bonds are considered the safest investment. Their prices tend to rise during market crashes, making them an excellent hedge.
- **Corporate Bonds**: High-quality corporate bonds offer higher yields than Treasuries but come with slightly more risk.
- **Municipal Bonds**: Tax-advantaged and relatively stable, these are ideal for investors in higher tax brackets.

- **Inflation-Protected Bonds**: Treasury Inflation-Protected Securities (TIPS) adjust their principal value based on inflation, protecting against rising prices.

3. Laddering Bonds

Bond laddering involves purchasing bonds with staggered maturities. This strategy ensures liquidity and reduces the risk of reinvesting at unfavorable rates. For example, you might buy bonds maturing in 1, 3, 5, and 10 years to hedge against changing interest rates.

4. Allocating Bonds in Your Portfolio

The proportion of bonds in your portfolio depends on your risk tolerance and investment horizon. Conservative investors or those nearing retirement often increase bond allocations to preserve capital.

Combining Hedging Strategies

The most effective hedging strategies often involve a combination of tools. For example:

- Use **put options** to protect against sudden stock declines while maintaining growth potential.
- Allocate a portion of your portfolio to **gold** to hedge against inflation and economic uncertainty.
- Invest in **bonds** for stability and income generation, ensuring your portfolio remains balanced during market turmoil.

Example Portfolio Allocation:

- 60% stocks (hedged with put options)
- 20% bonds (Treasuries and corporate bonds)

- 10% gold (via ETFs or physical assets)
- 10% cash (to capitalize on market opportunities during a downturn)

Risks of Hedging

While hedging provides protection, it's not without its drawbacks:

- **Cost**: Options premiums, gold storage fees, and low bond yields can erode returns.
- **Complexity**: Some strategies, like options trading, require expertise.
- **Over-Hedging**: Excessive hedging can limit upside potential and reduce portfolio growth.

Hedging in Action: A Case Study

During the 2008 financial crisis:

- Investors who held significant allocations in gold saw their portfolios outperform as gold prices soared by nearly 25%.
- Treasury bond prices rose sharply, offsetting losses in equities.
- Those who bought put options on major indices like the S&P 500 mitigated much of the market's decline.

This trifecta of options, gold, and bonds exemplifies how hedging can preserve wealth during severe downturns.

Emergency Funds and Liquidity Management

An essential cornerstone of financial stability—whether for individuals, families, or businesses—is having a robust emergency fund and a well-structured liquidity management plan. These safeguards ensure you're prepared to navigate unexpected financial disruptions, such as job loss, medical emergencies, or economic downturns, without resorting to high-interest debt or liquidating long-term investments. This chapter explores the importance of emergency funds, how to establish one, and strategies for effective liquidity management.

What is an Emergency Fund?

An emergency fund is a pool of readily accessible cash set aside specifically for unforeseen expenses. Unlike investments, which grow wealth over time, an emergency fund acts as a financial safety net, protecting you from the stress and consequences of unexpected financial shocks.

Why Do You Need an Emergency Fund?

1. **Peace of Mind**
   Knowing you have a cushion for emergencies reduces financial anxiety and allows you to focus on long-term goals without fear of derailing your plans.

2. **Avoiding Debt**
   Without an emergency fund, many people turn to credit cards or personal loans to cover unexpected expenses, leading to high-interest debt that can spiral out of control.

3. **Protecting Investments**
   An emergency fund prevents you from having to sell long-term investments during market downturns, preserving your portfolio's growth potential.

4. **Maintaining Financial Independence**
   Relying on others for financial help during emergencies can strain relationships. A solid emergency fund allows you to remain self-reliant.

How Much Should You Save?

The size of your emergency fund depends on your lifestyle, income stability, and financial obligations. A common guideline is:

- **3 to 6 months of essential expenses** for salaried individuals.
- **6 to 12 months of expenses** for freelancers, self-employed individuals, or those with irregular income.

Essential expenses include:

- Rent or mortgage payments.
- Utilities.
- Groceries and household necessities.
- Transportation costs.
- Insurance premiums.

Building an Emergency Fund

1. **Set a Target Amount**
   Calculate your monthly essential expenses and multiply them by the desired number of months (e.g., 3-6).

2. **Start Small and Scale Up**
   Begin by saving a small percentage of your income, such as 10-15%, and gradually increase the amount as your financial situation improves.

3. **Automate Savings**
   Set up automatic transfers to a dedicated emergency fund account. Automation ensures consistency and reduces the temptation to spend.

4. **Use Windfalls Wisely**
   Direct bonuses, tax refunds, or other unexpected income toward your emergency fund.

5. **Prioritize High-Interest Debt First**
   If you have high-interest debt, focus on paying it down while building a smaller emergency fund of $1,000–$2,000 for immediate needs.

Where to Keep Your Emergency Fund

Accessibility and safety are key factors in choosing where to store your emergency fund. Options include:

1. **High-Yield Savings Accounts**
   - These accounts offer better interest rates than traditional savings accounts while keeping funds easily accessible.

- Ensure the account is insured by the FDIC or an equivalent body.

2. **Money Market Accounts**
    - Money market accounts provide slightly higher returns and liquidity.
    - Some come with check-writing privileges for quick access.

3. **Cash Management Accounts (CMAs)**
    - Offered by brokerages, CMAs combine features of savings and checking accounts with competitive interest rates.

4. **Short-Term Certificates of Deposit (CDs)**
    - CDs with short maturity periods (3-12 months) offer higher interest rates than savings accounts. However, early withdrawals may incur penalties.

5. **Tiered Approach**
    - Consider splitting your fund into tiers:
        - **Tier 1**: Immediate access (savings account).
        - **Tier 2**: Short-term savings (money market or short-term CDs).

Liquidity Management

Liquidity refers to how quickly and easily you can access cash or assets without significant loss in value. Effective liquidity management ensures that you have enough liquid assets to cover short-term needs without jeopardizing your financial health.

Liquidity Strategies for Individuals

1. **Diversify Savings Accounts**
   Keep cash in multiple accessible accounts to avoid being caught off guard by transaction limits or access issues.

2. **Avoid Over-Saving in Low-Return Accounts**
   While liquidity is important, keeping too much in low-yield accounts can erode purchasing power due to inflation. Strike a balance between liquidity and returns.

3. **Maintain a Line of Credit**
   A personal line of credit can serve as a backup in extreme emergencies, offering quick access to funds at a lower interest rate than credit cards.

4. **Use Liquid Investments Sparingly**
   Investments like short-term bond funds or dividend-paying stocks provide liquidity with some growth potential but should only be considered after your core emergency fund is in place.

Liquidity Strategies for Businesses

1. **Cash Flow Forecasting**
   Regularly review cash flow projections to anticipate and address liquidity shortfalls.

2. **Establish a Cash Reserve**
   Similar to an individual emergency fund, businesses should maintain a reserve covering 3-6 months of operating expenses.

3. **Negotiate Credit Terms**
   Work with suppliers to secure favorable payment terms, improving cash flow flexibility.

4. **Use a Business Line of Credit**
   Keep a line of credit open for unforeseen expenses or short-term funding needs.

5. **Optimize Accounts Receivable**
   Reduce the time it takes to collect payments from clients by offering early payment discounts or using invoice factoring.

Common Mistakes to Avoid

1. **Using Emergency Funds for Non-Essential Expenses**
   Avoid dipping into your fund for discretionary purchases. Treat it as sacred money reserved for true emergencies.

2. **Underestimating Expenses**
   Review your budget periodically to ensure your emergency fund reflects changes in your cost of living.

3. **Ignoring Inflation**
   Keep your emergency fund in accounts that at least match the inflation rate to preserve purchasing power.

4. **Relying Solely on Credit**
   Credit cards or loans may not always be accessible

during economic downturns or personal financial crises.

Emergency Fund vs. Investment Liquidity

An emergency fund is distinct from liquid investments:

- **Emergency Fund**: Accessible, low-risk, and not tied to market performance.
- **Liquid Investments**: May include stocks or ETFs, but their value can fluctuate, making them less reliable in a financial emergency.

For example, selling stocks during a market downturn to cover an emergency locks in losses, whereas a cash-based fund shields you from market risks.

Case Study: The Role of Emergency Funds During a Crisis

During the COVID-19 pandemic, individuals and businesses with emergency funds fared better:

- **Individuals**: Those with 3-6 months' worth of expenses avoided defaulting on rent or loans when layoffs surged.
- **Businesses**: Companies with strong liquidity managed to retain employees and weather temporary revenue declines, emerging stronger post-crisis.

Conversely, those without emergency funds faced mounting debt and financial instability, underscoring the importance of preparedness.

Conclusion

An emergency fund and liquidity management plan are the bedrock of financial resilience. They ensure that life's unexpected events don't derail your long-term goals or force you into unwise financial decisions. By setting aside cash in secure, accessible accounts and managing liquidity effectively, you create a safety net that allows you to face any challenge with confidence and stability.

CHAPTER 8

TIMING THE MARKET: MYTH OR REALITY?

The idea of timing the market—the notion that one can predict market highs and lows with precision—is alluring. After all, who wouldn't want to sell just before a crash or buy at the exact bottom of a downturn? Yet, while this concept holds immense theoretical appeal, in practice, timing the market is one of the most challenging endeavors even for seasoned investors. This chapter explores why timing the market is more myth than reality, supported by historical evidence, psychological challenges, and practical constraints.

The Seduction of Certainty

Investors crave certainty, especially in the volatile world of the stock market. Headlines and financial analysts often fuel this desire, claiming to see signs of impending doom or recovery. The human brain is wired to seek patterns, and in the face of randomness, it tends to overinterpret data, mistaking correlation for causation.

Market predictions often fail because they are based on incomplete or misinterpreted information. Economic indicators, political events, and market trends do provide clues, but they rarely tell the full story. The sheer number of variables influencing market movements—from global trade dynamics to unexpected geopolitical crises—makes prediction a near-impossible task.

The History of Failed Predictions

History is littered with failed market predictions. Economists, fund managers, and financial gurus have often missed the mark, even when armed with advanced models and insider knowledge. Consider these examples:

- **The Dot-Com Bubble**: In the late 1990s, many analysts believed that technology stocks would continue their meteoric rise indefinitely. When the bubble burst in 2000, countless investors were caught off guard.

- **The 2008 Financial Crisis**: While there were warnings about the housing bubble, few anticipated the systemic collapse of major financial institutions or the global ramifications.

- **The COVID-19 Crash of 2020**: The speed and scale of the pandemic-induced crash surprised most experts. While some rebounded quickly, others exited the market in panic, missing out on the rapid recovery.

Even when predictions about a crash prove accurate, the timing is often wrong. Markets can remain irrationally overvalued for years before correcting, leaving investors who act too early sidelined as others reap the rewards of prolonged bull runs.

The Psychological Toll of Market Timing

Timing the market isn't just a logistical challenge; it's a psychological minefield. Fear and greed dominate decision-making, leading investors to sell prematurely or hold on for too long. The emotional rollercoaster of attempting to time the market can cause even the most disciplined investors to make costly mistakes.

- **Fear of Missing Out (FOMO)**: During bull markets, FOMO drives investors to chase rising stocks, often buying at inflated prices. Conversely, during downturns, fear of further losses may lead them to sell at the worst possible time.

- **Confirmation Bias**: Investors often seek out information that aligns with their beliefs, ignoring evidence that contradicts their predictions. This bias can blind them to changing market conditions.

- **Herd Mentality**: The tendency to follow the crowd exacerbates poor timing decisions. When everyone is selling, the pressure to join the herd can be overwhelming, even when it goes against sound investment principles.

Practical Constraints of Market Timing

Even if one could predict a crash, executing the perfect trade at the right time is fraught with practical challenges:

- **Market Efficiency**: Modern financial markets are highly efficient, meaning that prices often reflect all available information. By the time a crash is visible, it's often too late to act.

- **Transaction Costs**: Frequent buying and selling to time the market can erode returns through brokerage fees, taxes, and other costs.

- **Opportunity Costs**: Investors who sell in anticipation of a crash may miss out on continued gains if the market doesn't decline as expected. Over time, staying invested often outperforms market-timing attempts.

What the Experts Say

Notable investors and financial theorists have consistently advised against timing the market. Warren Buffett, one of the most successful investors of all time, famously said, *"The stock market is a device for transferring money from the impatient to the patient."* His strategy—buying quality assets and holding them for the long term—has outperformed countless attempts at market timing.

John Bogle, the founder of Vanguard and a proponent of index investing, emphasized the importance of time *in* the market rather than timing the market. His data-backed approach showed that long-term investors who remained consistently invested in the market fared better than those who tried to jump in and out.

The Case for Staying Invested

Rather than attempting to time the market, investors are better served by focusing on long-term strategies:

1. **Diversification**: Spread investments across asset classes, industries, and geographies to reduce risk.

2. **Asset Allocation**: Maintain a balanced portfolio tailored to your risk tolerance and financial goals.

3. **Systematic Investing**: Use dollar-cost averaging to invest consistently, regardless of market conditions.

4. **Rebalancing**: Periodically adjust your portfolio to maintain your desired asset allocation.

These strategies help mitigate the impact of market volatility without the need for precise timing.

The Dangers of Trying to Time the Market Versus Staying Invested

The allure of trying to time the market is undeniable. Who wouldn't want to sell just before a downturn and re-enter the market at its lowest point, maximizing gains and avoiding losses? However, while this idea sounds logical in theory, it's incredibly difficult to execute in practice. Attempting to time the market can lead to costly mistakes, missed opportunities, and long-term underperformance. This chapter explores the dangers of market timing and highlights the benefits of staying invested for the long haul.

The Illusion of Control

Market timing gives investors the illusion of control in an unpredictable environment. This sense of control is comforting, particularly during volatile periods when the fear of losses looms large. However, market movements are influenced by countless factors, including economic data, geopolitical events, investor sentiment, and even unexpected disasters. Predicting these events with accuracy and timing trades accordingly is nearly impossible.

Even professional investors armed with advanced models and years of experience struggle to time the market consistently. Individual investors face an even steeper challenge, often falling prey to emotional decision-making and cognitive biases.

The Real Cost of Being Out of the Market

One of the most significant dangers of market timing is the risk of being out of the market during its best-performing days. Historical data shows that the stock market's biggest gains often occur during brief, unpredictable periods. Missing just a handful of these days can have a devastating impact on long-term returns.

For example, consider the S&P 500's performance over a 20-year period:

- Staying fully invested from 2003 to 2023 would have yielded an average annual return of approximately 10%.

- Missing just the 10 best-performing days would have reduced that return to around 5%.

- Missing the 20 best days would drop the return further to less than 2%, barely keeping pace with inflation.

The problem? Those best-performing days often occur during periods of extreme volatility, when many investors are on the sidelines, waiting for clarity.

Emotional Pitfalls of Market Timing

Market timing requires not just one correct decision but two: knowing when to sell and when to buy back in. Both decisions are fraught with emotional challenges that can lead to costly mistakes.

1. **Fear and Greed**: These emotions dominate market timing. Fear leads investors to sell during downturns, locking in losses, while greed can cause them to buy into overheated markets at their peak.

2. **Herd Mentality**: Investors often follow the crowd, selling during market panics and buying during euphoric rallies. This behavior exacerbates poor timing decisions.

3. **Paralysis by Analysis**: Overanalyzing market data can lead to hesitation, causing investors to miss opportunities while waiting for the "perfect" time to act.

4. **Overconfidence**: Some investors believe they can outsmart the market, but overconfidence often leads to rash decisions and increased risk-taking.

The Benefits of Staying Invested

While market timing is fraught with challenges, staying invested has proven to be a more reliable strategy for building wealth. Here's why:

1. **Compounding Over Time**: Staying invested allows your money to benefit from the power of compounding. Even modest returns can grow significantly over decades.

2. **Market Recovery**: History has shown that markets recover from downturns. Investors who remain patient and stay invested are well-positioned to benefit from the eventual rebound.

3. **Eliminating Guesswork**: By staying invested, you eliminate the need to guess market tops and bottoms. This approach reduces stress and the likelihood of making emotional decisions.

4. **Predictable Returns**: Over the long term, stock markets have delivered consistent positive returns, despite short-term volatility. Staying invested ensures you capture this growth.

A Tale of Two Investors

To illustrate the dangers of market timing versus staying invested, consider two hypothetical investors, Sarah and John.

- **Sarah, the Market Timer**: Sarah attempts to time the market, selling her investments during downturns and buying back in when she feels confident. Unfortunately, her decisions are often influenced by fear and news headlines. She misses key recovery periods and incurs transaction costs. Over 20 years, her portfolio grows at an average annual rate of 4%.

- **John, the Patient Investor**: John adopts a buy-and-hold strategy, staying invested through market ups and downs. Despite enduring several bear markets, he benefits from the market's long-term growth. Over the same 20 years, his portfolio grows at an average annual rate of 8%, significantly outpacing Sarah's returns.

This example highlights the high cost of market timing and the rewards of staying the course.

Practical Strategies for Staying Invested

To maximize the benefits of staying invested while managing risk, consider these strategies:

1. **Dollar-Cost Averaging**: Invest a fixed amount regularly, regardless of market conditions. This approach reduces the impact of market volatility and eliminates the need for timing decisions.

2. **Diversification**: Spread your investments across asset classes, industries, and geographies to reduce risk.

3. **Rebalancing**: Periodically adjust your portfolio to maintain your desired asset allocation. This ensures you buy low and sell high without attempting to time the market.

4. **Emergency Fund**: Maintain a cash reserve to cover unexpected expenses. This reduces the temptation to sell investments during downturns.

5. **Long-Term Perspective**: Focus on your financial goals and the big picture. Remember that short-term volatility is a normal part of investing.

Conclusion

The dangers of trying to time the market far outweigh the potential rewards. While the idea of avoiding losses and maximizing gains is appealing, the reality is that market timing is incredibly difficult and often counterproductive. Staying invested, on the other hand, provides a proven path to long-term wealth creation. By maintaining discipline, avoiding emotional decisions, and focusing on a diversified, long-term strategy, investors can achieve their financial goals without falling into the pitfalls of market timing. In the end, time in the market beats timing the market every time.

CHAPTER 9

STRATEGIES FOR PROFITING DURING AND AFTER A CRASH

Short Selling: Risks and Rewards

Stock market crashes are often seen as catastrophic events, sending investors into panic mode. However, these moments of financial turbulence can also present unique opportunities for those who understand how to navigate them. One such strategy is **short selling**, a technique that allows investors to profit from declining stock prices. While the concept may sound simple, short selling comes with significant risks and requires a deep understanding of market dynamics.

Understanding Short Selling

Short selling is the process of selling shares you don't own, with the intention of buying them back later at a lower price. Here's how it works:

1. **Borrowing Shares**: You borrow shares from a broker, typically for a fee.

2. **Selling the Shares**: You sell the borrowed shares at the current market price.

3. **Buying Back the Shares**: You aim to repurchase the shares at a lower price to return them to the broker.

4. **Pocketing the Difference**: If the stock price drops, you profit from the difference between the selling price and the buying price, minus fees and interest.

For example, if you short sell 100 shares of a company at $50 per share and later buy them back at $30, you make a profit of $20 per share, or $2,000 (before costs).

The Rewards of Short Selling

Short selling offers distinct advantages during a market crash:

1. **Profiting in Bear Markets**: While most investors experience losses during a downturn, short sellers can profit as prices fall.

2. **Hedging Against Losses**: Short selling can be used to hedge against losses in a long portfolio. For instance, if you hold shares in an industry that is vulnerable during a crash, shorting related stocks can offset some of your losses.

3. **Market Correction Opportunities**: Overvalued stocks often come under pressure during a crash. Short sellers can identify these inflated stocks and capitalize on their decline.

The Risks of Short Selling

Short selling is not for the faint-hearted. The potential for losses is theoretically unlimited, as there's no limit to how high a stock price can rise. Here are the main risks:

1. **Unlimited Losses**: Unlike a traditional investment where the maximum loss is your initial investment, short selling exposes you to unlimited losses if the stock price skyrockets. For example, if a stock you shorted at $50 surges to $200, your losses are enormous.

2. **Margin Calls**: Since short selling is done on margin (borrowed money), brokers may require you to deposit additional funds if the stock price moves against you. This is known as a margin call.

3. **Short Squeezes**: If a heavily shorted stock experiences a sudden price surge, it can force short sellers to buy back shares quickly to cover their positions, further driving up the price in a phenomenon known as a short squeeze.

4. **Borrowing Costs**: You must pay fees to borrow the shares, which can add up, especially if the stock is hard to borrow or the short position is held for a long time.

The Ethics of Short Selling

Short selling often attracts criticism, as it involves profiting from a company's misfortune. Critics argue that short sellers contribute to panic during market downturns. However, others believe short selling plays a critical role in keeping markets efficient by exposing overvalued stocks and corporate fraud. For instance, short sellers were instrumental in uncovering scandals such as Enron and Wirecard.

How to Succeed with Short Selling

Short selling requires a disciplined and well-researched approach. Here are some key strategies to improve your chances of success:

1. **Target Overvalued Stocks**: Look for stocks with inflated valuations, weak fundamentals, or industries facing significant headwinds. These are prime candidates for price declines during a crash.

2. **Use Technical Analysis**: Technical indicators like moving averages and relative strength index (RSI) can help identify overbought conditions, signaling potential short-selling opportunities.

3. **Diversify Your Short Positions**: Avoid putting all your bets on a single stock. Diversify across multiple sectors to reduce the risk of a short squeeze or unexpected news impacting your position.

4. **Set Stop-Loss Orders**: To manage risk, always set stop-loss orders to limit potential losses if the stock price moves against you.

5. **Stay Informed**: Monitor market conditions and news related to the stocks you've shorted. Events such as earnings reports, mergers, or government interventions can drastically affect stock prices.

Alternatives to Short Selling

If the risks of short selling seem too high, consider these alternatives:

1. **Put Options**: Buying put options gives you the right to sell a stock at a predetermined price. Unlike short selling, your maximum loss is limited to the premium paid for the option.

2. **Inverse ETFs**: Exchange-Traded Funds (ETFs) that move inversely to the market or specific sectors allow you to profit from declines without directly shorting stocks.

3. **Cash Positions**: Holding cash during a crash can provide liquidity and the ability to buy undervalued stocks when the market stabilizes.

Case Study: The 2008 Financial Crisis

During the 2008 financial crisis, savvy short sellers like Michael Burry and hedge funds such as Paulson & Co. made billions by betting against the subprime mortgage market. They identified weaknesses in mortgage-backed securities and used a combination of short selling and credit default swaps to profit as the market collapsed.

Their success highlights the importance of research, patience, and the willingness to go against the crowd—traits that all successful short sellers possess.

Buying High-Quality Stocks at a Discount

One of the most effective strategies during a stock market crash is to seize the opportunity to buy high-quality stocks at discounted prices. Market downturns, often fueled by fear and panic, create a temporary disconnection between a company's intrinsic value and its market price. For savvy investors, these periods of volatility can serve as a golden ticket to accumulate robust stocks that are temporarily undervalued.

In this chapter, we'll explore how to identify high-quality stocks, evaluate their intrinsic value, and navigate the risks and rewards of buying during a downturn.

Why Crashes Offer Buying Opportunities

Market crashes often lead to indiscriminate selling as investors rush to liquidate their positions. This mass exodus isn't always driven by the fundamentals of the underlying businesses but by fear, liquidity needs, or speculative panic. As a result, even fundamentally strong companies can see their stock prices plummet, creating an opportunity for long-term investors to buy these assets at a discount.

Consider the 2008 financial crisis: blue-chip stocks like Apple, Amazon, and Berkshire Hathaway saw significant declines, only to recover and reach new highs in the years that followed. Those who bought these stocks during the crash reaped substantial returns.

What Defines a High-Quality Stock?

Before investing in a market downturn, it's crucial to identify stocks that are worth buying. High-quality stocks share certain key characteristics:

1. **Strong Financials**: Look for companies with low debt, healthy cash reserves, and consistent revenue and profit growth.
2. **Competitive Advantage**: Companies with a unique product, service, or market position are more likely to withstand economic downturns.
3. **Stable Management**: A strong, experienced leadership team can navigate challenging times effectively.

4. **Resilient Industry**: Companies in essential sectors like healthcare, consumer staples, and utilities tend to be less affected by market crashes.

5. **History of Performance**: Check if the company has a track record of surviving and thriving after previous market downturns.

How to Identify Discounted Stocks

Identifying high-quality stocks at a discount involves understanding both the company's intrinsic value and the price it's trading at during the crash. Here's how to approach it:

1. Intrinsic Value Assessment

Intrinsic value is the true worth of a company based on its fundamentals, irrespective of its current market price. You can calculate it using:

- **Discounted Cash Flow (DCF) Analysis**: This method estimates the present value of a company's future cash flows.

- **Price-to-Earnings (P/E) Ratio**: Compare the company's P/E ratio to its historical average or industry peers to determine if it's undervalued.

- **Book Value**: Evaluate the company's assets minus its liabilities. If the stock is trading below its book value, it could indicate a bargain.

2. Monitor the Price Drop

A stock that has dropped significantly may be discounted, but ensure the drop is due to market conditions and not company-specific issues. Compare the stock's current price to its historical highs and lows.

3. Look for Dividend Safety

Companies that consistently pay dividends, even during tough times, often signal financial strength and stability. Ensure their dividend payout ratio (dividends as a percentage of earnings) is sustainable.

Strategies for Buying During a Crash

1. Focus on Blue-Chip Stocks

Blue-chip stocks are shares of large, established, and financially sound companies with a history of weathering economic storms. Examples include companies like Johnson & Johnson, Microsoft, and Coca-Cola.

2. Adopt a Long-Term Perspective

Market crashes can last months or even years, but history shows that markets eventually recover. Adopt a mindset of patience, aiming for returns over the long term rather than quick profits.

3. Use Dollar-Cost Averaging

Instead of trying to time the market, invest a fixed amount of money at regular intervals. This approach reduces the risk of buying all at once at a high price and allows you to benefit from further declines.

4. Build a Watchlist

Create a list of high-quality stocks you want to own before a crash occurs. Monitor their performance and valuation regularly so you're prepared to act when the opportunity arises.

5. Buy in Tranches

Avoid deploying all your capital at once. Buying in tranches—small portions of your total budget—allows you to take advantage of further price declines.

Risks to Watch For

While buying high-quality stocks during a crash can be lucrative, it's not without risks:

1. **Catching a Falling Knife**
   Just because a stock is trading at a lower price doesn't mean it can't fall further. Ensure the fundamentals remain strong before investing.

2. **Sector-Specific Crashes**
   Sometimes, entire industries face structural challenges (e.g., brick-and-mortar retail in the face of e-commerce). Avoid companies in declining sectors, even if their stocks seem discounted.

3. **Liquidity Issues**
   Ensure you have enough cash reserves to manage personal needs and potential market opportunities. Avoid overcommitting during uncertain times.

4. **Emotional Investing**
   Fear and greed can cloud judgment during a crash. Stick to your strategy and avoid impulsive decisions.

Case Study: Amazon During the Dot-Com Bubble

During the dot-com crash of the early 2000s, Amazon's stock price plummeted from over $100 per share to under $10. While many investors wrote off the company as a failed tech experiment, those who recognized Amazon's strong fundamentals and long-term potential saw an opportunity to invest at a massive discount.

Fast-forward to today, and Amazon has grown into one of the world's largest companies, with its stock price multiplying hundreds of times since the crash. This underscores the importance of identifying businesses with solid fundamentals during times of market distress.

Investing in ETFs and Index Funds Post-Crash

Market crashes often shake investor confidence, leaving many hesitant to re-enter the market. However, for those who prefer a diversified, lower-risk approach to capitalizing on post-crash recoveries, investing in **ETFs (Exchange-Traded Funds)** and **index funds** can be a smart choice. These investment vehicles provide exposure to broad markets or specific sectors, offering a balanced and cost-effective way to rebuild wealth after a downturn.

In this chapter, we'll explore why ETFs and index funds are effective post-crash investment tools, how to choose the right funds, and strategies for maximizing returns while minimizing risks.

Why ETFs and Index Funds Shine Post-Crash

During a market crash, individual stocks can experience dramatic swings, often making them a risky bet. ETFs and index funds, by contrast, offer the benefits of diversification and lower volatility, making them particularly appealing during uncertain times.

1. **Diversification**:
   These funds hold a basket of securities, spreading risk across multiple companies, sectors, or even countries. This reduces the impact of poor performance by any single stock.

2. **Market Recovery Potential**:
   History shows that markets tend to recover after crashes. ETFs and index funds tied to major indices (e.g., S&P 500, NASDAQ) allow investors to participate in the overall recovery without needing to pick individual winners.

3. **Cost Efficiency**:
   Both ETFs and index funds typically have low expense ratios compared to actively managed funds, meaning more of your money goes toward generating returns.

4. **Ease of Investment**:
   These funds are simple to understand and require no extensive research into individual companies. They are ideal for beginner investors or those with limited time to manage their portfolios.

5. **Flexibility**:
   ETFs, in particular, trade on stock exchanges like individual stocks, allowing you to buy or sell them throughout the trading day. This provides liquidity and flexibility in your investment decisions.

How to Choose the Right ETFs and Index Funds Post-Crash

Not all ETFs and index funds are created equal. Selecting the right ones requires evaluating your financial goals, risk tolerance, and market conditions.

1. Broad Market ETFs and Index Funds

- **Examples**: S&P 500 Index Funds (e.g., Vanguard S&P 500 ETF), Total Market ETFs (e.g., iShares Russell 3000 ETF).
- **Why Choose Them**: These funds track major indices, offering exposure to a wide range of companies. They are ideal for participating in a broad market recovery.

2. Sector-Specific ETFs

- **Examples**: Technology ETFs (e.g., Invesco QQQ), Healthcare ETFs (e.g., Vanguard Health Care ETF).
- **Why Choose Them**: Some sectors recover faster or outperform others post-crash. For example, technology and healthcare often lead recoveries due to innovation and necessity.

3. Dividend-Focused ETFs

- **Examples**: Vanguard Dividend Appreciation ETF, Schwab U.S. Dividend Equity ETF.
- **Why Choose Them**: Dividend-paying stocks are typically more stable and provide income during recovery periods.

4. International ETFs

- **Examples**: iShares MSCI Emerging Markets ETF, Vanguard FTSE Developed Markets ETF.

- **Why Choose Them**: Diversifying globally can help balance exposure, especially if certain international markets are recovering faster than domestic ones.

5. Bond ETFs

- **Examples**: iShares Core U.S. Aggregate Bond ETF, Vanguard Total Bond Market ETF.

- **Why Choose Them**: Bond ETFs can provide stability and consistent income as part of a balanced portfolio during volatile recovery periods.

Strategies for Investing in ETFs and Index Funds Post-Crash

1. Dollar-Cost Averaging

Instead of investing a lump sum, spread your investments over time. This approach allows you to buy more shares when prices are low and fewer when prices are high, reducing the impact of market volatility.

2. Focus on Recovery Sectors

Identify sectors that are likely to rebound strongly based on the nature of the crash. For example, technology and consumer discretionary sectors often bounce back quickly after economic recessions.

3. Rebalance Your Portfolio

As the market recovers, some ETFs or funds in your portfolio may outperform others. Periodically rebalance your investments to maintain your desired allocation and risk level.

4. Leverage Low Fees

Choose funds with low expense ratios to maximize your long-term returns. Every percentage point saved on fees can significantly impact your overall wealth.

5. Combine Active and Passive Approaches

While index funds and ETFs are inherently passive investments, consider complementing them with active strategies, such as targeting undervalued individual stocks, to boost returns.

The Role of Patience and Discipline

Post-crash recoveries are rarely linear. Markets often experience short-term volatility, including dead cat bounces and secondary dips, before stabilizing. ETFs and index funds require a long-term commitment to reap their full benefits. Avoid the temptation to sell prematurely during temporary downturns, and trust the recovery process.

Real-World Examples

1. S&P 500 Recovery After the 2008 Crisis

After the 2008 financial crisis, the S&P 500 dropped nearly 50% from its peak. Investors who bought S&P 500 index funds during the crash saw massive gains as the index rebounded, eventually reaching new highs.

2. The Tech Sector's Recovery Post-Dot-Com Crash

ETFs like the Invesco QQQ, which tracks the NASDAQ-100, provided exposure to leading tech companies such as Apple and Microsoft. Investors who bought tech-focused ETFs during the dot-com crash reaped substantial rewards as technology companies grew in prominence.

3. COVID-19 Pandemic Crash and Recovery

The COVID-19 pandemic triggered a sharp market decline in early 2020. Broad market ETFs like the Vanguard Total Stock Market ETF (VTI) and sector-specific ETFs like healthcare and technology funds rebounded strongly within months, rewarding patient investors.

Advantages and Risks of ETFs and Index Funds Post-Crash

Advantages:

1. **Broad Exposure**: Reduces the risk associated with individual stock selection.

2. **Lower Costs**: Minimal management fees compared to actively managed funds.

3. **Simplicity**: Easy to understand and manage, even for novice investors.

Risks:

1. **Market Correlation**: If the broader market or sector remains depressed, ETFs tracking those areas will underperform.

2. **Limited Upside**: Unlike individual stocks, ETFs and index funds rarely deliver outsized gains, as they track the average performance of their holdings.

3. **Sector-Specific Volatility**: Sector ETFs can still be subject to significant volatility if the recovery is uneven across industries.

Conclusion

Investing in ETFs and index funds post-crash is an excellent strategy for both beginner and experienced investors seeking to benefit from market recoveries without taking on excessive risk. Their inherent diversification, cost efficiency, and alignment with long-term market trends make them a cornerstone of any well-rounded investment portfolio. By focusing on high-quality funds, employing disciplined strategies, and maintaining patience, you can position yourself to turn the aftermath of a crash into a wealth-building opportunity.

CHAPTER 10

PREPARING FOR THE NEXT CRASH

Recognizing Red Flags in the Market

The stock market operates in cycles of booms and busts. While the precise timing of a crash remains elusive, there are often warning signs that savvy investors can recognize. Preparing for the next crash isn't about predicting when it will happen; it's about identifying potential red flags, staying informed, and having a clear strategy. By doing so, you can mitigate risks, protect your investments, and even capitalize on opportunities during turbulent times.

1. Unprecedented Market Euphoria

When markets soar to new heights, it's easy to get caught up in the excitement. News outlets trumpet record-breaking highs, and everyday investors begin to believe that the market will only go up. This widespread optimism can be a sign of an overheated market.

Red flags include:

- **Skyrocketing Valuations**: Stocks trading at price-to-earnings (P/E) ratios far above historical averages.
- **Speculative Buying**: A surge in speculative assets, such as meme stocks or cryptocurrencies, with little intrinsic value.
- **Uninformed Investors Entering the Market**: Stories of people with no prior experience investing significant amounts based on hype.

2. Excessive Leverage and Debt

Leverage amplifies both gains and losses. During bull markets, investors and companies often take on excessive debt to capitalize on rising prices. However, when the market turns, this leverage can quickly spiral out of control, leading to forced selling and widespread panic.

Key indicators:

- **Margin Debt at Record Levels**: An increase in margin borrowing to buy stocks can signal overconfidence.
- **Corporate Debt Bubbles**: Companies with weak financials issuing massive amounts of debt, particularly junk bonds.
- **Rising Debt-to-GDP Ratios**: A sign that governments or economies are overly reliant on borrowing to sustain growth.

3. Deteriorating Economic Indicators

The stock market is not the economy, but the two are closely connected. If key economic indicators begin to show signs of weakness, it may suggest trouble ahead for the markets.

Keep an eye on:

- **Rising Unemployment**: A slowing job market can reduce consumer spending, which fuels much of the economy.

- **Declining Consumer Confidence**: If consumers feel uncertain about their financial future, they may cut back on spending, leading to slower growth.

- **Inverted Yield Curve**: When short-term interest rates exceed long-term rates, it's often a precursor to a recession.

4. Geopolitical Tensions

Markets thrive on stability. When global events disrupt this stability, they can trigger sudden and severe market reactions.

Potential triggers include:

- **Trade Wars**: Tariffs and sanctions can disrupt global supply chains, impacting corporate profits.

- **Military Conflicts**: Heightened tensions or outright wars can shake investor confidence.

- **Political Uncertainty**: Elections, policy changes, or leadership crises in major economies can lead to volatility.

5. Central Bank Actions and Interest Rates

Central banks play a critical role in maintaining economic stability. When they shift monetary policies, it often has a ripple effect on the markets.

Red flags to monitor:

- **Rapid Interest Rate Hikes**: Central banks raising rates aggressively to combat inflation can cool the economy and hurt stock valuations.
- **Quantitative Tightening (QT)**: The reversal of quantitative easing, where central banks reduce their balance sheets, can drain liquidity from markets.
- **Rising Inflation**: Persistent inflation can erode purchasing power and prompt central banks to tighten monetary policy further.

6. Market Breadth and Divergence

Market breadth refers to the number of stocks participating in a market's advance or decline. When only a few large companies drive gains while the rest lag, it may indicate underlying weakness.

Signs to watch for:

- **Narrow Leadership**: A handful of stocks, typically in the same sector (e.g., technology), accounting for most of the market's gains.
- **Sector Divergence**: Certain sectors underperforming significantly while others seem overheated.

7. Corporate Earnings Declines

Stock prices are ultimately tied to earnings. If companies begin reporting declining profits or issuing lower guidance, it may signal that the market's growth is unsustainable.

Indicators include:

- **Earnings Misses**: Companies consistently failing to meet Wall Street expectations.
- **Reduced Guidance**: Warnings from CEOs about slower growth ahead.
- **Shrinking Margins**: Rising costs cutting into profits, especially in sectors with high exposure to raw material prices.

8. Behavioral Signals in the Market

Investor behavior often provides valuable insights into potential market reversals. Excess greed or fear can distort prices and signal turning points.

Behavioral red flags:

- **Fear of Missing Out (FOMO)**: Investors rushing into the market due to hype, not fundamentals.
- **Herd Mentality**: A lack of contrarian thinking, with most participants chasing the same trends.
- **Increased Volatility**: Spikes in the VIX (volatility index) can indicate heightened market anxiety.

9. Historical Patterns and Cycles

While history doesn't repeat itself exactly, it often rhymes. Studying past market crashes can help identify patterns that may reoccur.

Learn from:

- **Excessive Speculation**: As seen in the dot-com bubble.

- **Housing Market Vulnerabilities**: As witnessed in the 2008 financial crisis.

- **Sector Bubbles**: Such as the overreliance on a single sector, like energy in the 1970s or tech in 2000.

Preparing for the Crash

Recognizing red flags is only part of the equation. You must also take proactive steps to prepare for a crash:

1. **Diversify Your Portfolio**: Avoid overexposure to a single sector or asset class.

2. **Maintain an Emergency Fund**: Ensure you have liquidity to navigate financial downturns.

3. **Reduce Leverage**: Avoid excessive borrowing to minimize potential losses.

4. **Stay Disciplined**: Stick to your long-term investment strategy and avoid panic selling.

5. **Build a Watchlist**: Identify undervalued stocks or sectors that you can invest in during the downturn.

By staying vigilant and prepared, you can weather the storm of a market crash and emerge stronger, leveraging opportunities that others may overlook. In every crisis lies the seed of potential growth—if you are ready to act.

Building a Solid Investment Plan with Contingencies

Investing is a journey filled with opportunities and risks. While the rewards can be significant, unexpected challenges, such as market downturns, economic crises, or personal financial emergencies, can derail even the best-laid plans.

Building a solid investment plan with contingencies ensures you're prepared for uncertainty and can navigate challenges while staying on track toward your financial goals.

This chapter explores the essential components of creating an investment strategy that includes safeguards for unforeseen circumstances.

---

1. Define Clear Investment Goals

The foundation of a strong investment plan lies in defining your objectives. Without a clear understanding of your goals, you risk making impulsive decisions that can hinder your progress.

Steps to define goals:

- **Short-Term Goals**: These might include saving for a home, starting a business, or funding education.
- **Medium-Term Goals**: Examples include building a retirement fund, paying off significant debts, or creating a safety net.
- **Long-Term Goals**: These often involve financial independence, legacy planning, or wealth generation for future generations.

Each goal should be **SMART**: Specific, Measurable, Achievable, Relevant, and Time-bound.

2. Diversify Your Investments

Diversification is a cornerstone of a resilient investment plan. Spreading your investments across different asset classes, sectors, and geographies reduces risk by minimizing the impact of any single underperforming asset.

Key elements of diversification:

- **Asset Classes**: Allocate funds among stocks, bonds, real estate, and commodities.

- **Geographic Exposure**: Invest in both domestic and international markets.

- **Sector Allocation**: Avoid overconcentration in one industry, even if it seems promising.

- **Alternative Investments**: Consider options like private equity, REITs (real estate investment trusts), or cryptocurrency (if aligned with your risk tolerance).

3. Assess and Manage Risk

Every investment carries risk. A solid plan requires you to assess your risk tolerance—your ability and willingness to endure market fluctuations—and align your portfolio accordingly.

Risk management strategies:

- **Know Your Risk Profile**: Are you conservative, moderate, or aggressive? Your profile will shape your portfolio.

- **Rebalance Regularly**: Periodically adjust your asset allocation to maintain your desired level of risk.

- **Limit High-Risk Investments**: Allocate only a small portion of your portfolio to speculative assets.

4. Create an Emergency Fund

An emergency fund acts as a financial cushion during unexpected situations, such as job loss, medical emergencies, or market downturns. Without one, you might be forced to liquidate investments at inopportune times.

How to build and maintain an emergency fund:

- **Set a Target**: Aim for three to six months' worth of living expenses.
- **Choose Liquid Assets**: Keep this fund in easily accessible accounts like savings accounts or money market funds.
- **Avoid Risky Investments**: Your emergency fund should prioritize stability over returns.

5. Establish Contingencies for Market Downturns

Market corrections and crashes are inevitable. Preparing for these events ensures you remain calm and strategic during turbulent times.

Contingency strategies:

- **Cash Reserve for Investments**: Maintain a portion of your portfolio in cash to capitalize on buying opportunities during downturns.
- **Stop-Loss Orders**: Use stop-loss mechanisms to automatically sell assets if their value drops beyond a certain point, limiting potential losses.

- **Focus on Defensive Sectors**: Allocate funds to sectors like healthcare, utilities, or consumer staples, which tend to be less volatile during recessions.
- **Stay the Course**: Avoid panic selling. Remember, market downturns are often followed by recoveries.

6. Plan for Personal Life Changes

Your financial circumstances can change due to factors such as marriage, having children, career transitions, or unexpected health issues. A robust plan includes contingencies for these life events.

Tips for adaptability:

- **Review Your Plan Regularly**: Reassess your investment strategy annually or after major life events.
- **Insurance Coverage**: Protect your family with life, health, and disability insurance.
- **Build Flexibility**: Include liquid investments that can be accessed if needed without penalties.

7. Incorporate Tax-Efficient Strategies

Taxes can significantly impact your investment returns. A solid plan minimizes tax liabilities while maximizing growth.

Tax-efficient tips:

- **Utilize Tax-Advantaged Accounts**: Contribute to retirement accounts like 401(k)s or IRAs, which offer tax benefits.

- **Harvest Tax Losses**: Offset capital gains by selling underperforming investments.
- **Dividend Reinvestment**: Consider reinvesting dividends into tax-advantaged accounts.
- **Understand Tax Implications**: Be aware of long-term versus short-term capital gains taxes and plan accordingly.

8. Create a Crisis Action Plan

Unexpected crises, whether personal or economic, require a pre-determined action plan. This ensures you respond rationally rather than emotionally.

Elements of a crisis plan:

- **Predefine Exit Points**: Decide in advance at what loss level you'll sell specific investments.
- **Emergency Contacts**: Work with a trusted financial advisor or accountant to navigate crises.
- **Scenario Analysis**: Run "what-if" scenarios to understand potential risks and outcomes.
- **Prioritize Essentials**: During a financial crisis, prioritize covering basic expenses over maintaining non-essential investments.

9. Automate and Simplify

Automation reduces the likelihood of emotional decision-making and ensures consistency.

Automating your plan:

- **Automatic Contributions**: Set up recurring transfers to investment accounts.
- **Dollar-Cost Averaging (DCA)**: Invest a fixed amount regularly, regardless of market conditions, to mitigate timing risk.
- **Set Alerts**: Use tools to notify you of significant changes in portfolio performance or market conditions.

10. Monitor and Adjust Over Time

Markets and life circumstances evolve. A strong investment plan is dynamic, adapting to new information and conditions.

How to stay on track:

- **Quarterly Reviews**: Assess your portfolio performance and realign it with your goals.
- **Benchmark Against Goals**: Ensure your investments are progressing toward your objectives.
- **Stay Educated**: Keep up with market trends, economic indicators, and financial news.
- **Consult Experts**: Seek advice from financial planners or advisors for major adjustments.

Educating Yourself Continuously About Market Trends

The stock market is dynamic, influenced by a multitude of factors ranging from economic indicators to geopolitical events. To stay ahead, investors must commit to lifelong learning, staying informed about market trends, and adapting their strategies to the ever-changing financial landscape. The more knowledge you have, the better equipped you are to make informed decisions that minimize risk and maximize returns.

In this chapter, we explore the importance of continuous education and how to stay updated on market trends effectively.

1. The Importance of Continuous Learning

Investing isn't a one-time decision; it's a process that evolves with the market. Markets react to new information, technological advancements, political shifts, and macroeconomic changes. Continuous learning allows you to:

- Adapt to changes in the market environment.
- Recognize emerging opportunities early.
- Avoid costly mistakes by staying informed about risks.
- Refine and improve your investment strategy over time.

The world of investing rewards those who commit to understanding its complexities and penalties for those who remain stagnant.

2. Sources of Reliable Information

Staying informed begins with identifying credible and diverse sources of information.

Recommended sources:

- **Financial News Platforms**: Follow reputable outlets such as Bloomberg, CNBC, Reuters, and The Wall Street Journal for daily updates.

- **Market Research Reports**: Access reports from firms like Morningstar, McKinsey, or Deloitte for in-depth analyses.

- **Earnings Reports**: Read quarterly and annual reports of companies you're invested in or interested in.

- **Central Bank Communications**: Monitor updates from institutions like the Federal Reserve or the European Central Bank to understand monetary policy changes.

- **Podcasts and Webinars**: Listen to industry experts discuss trends, forecasts, and strategies.

- **Books and Journals**: Deepen your understanding of investment principles by reading books by experts like Benjamin Graham, Peter Lynch, or Ray Dalio.

Online tools:

- **Market Data Platforms**: Websites like Yahoo Finance, Google Finance, or Investing.com provide real-time updates.

- **Professional Networking Sites**: Platforms like LinkedIn or Seeking Alpha allow you to connect with industry professionals and follow thought leaders.

- **Educational Platforms**: Courses on Coursera, Udemy, or Khan Academy offer structured learning on financial topics.

3. Understanding Key Market Indicators

To interpret market trends effectively, familiarize yourself with key economic and financial indicators:

Macro Indicators:

- **GDP Growth Rates**: Signals the overall health of the economy.
- **Inflation Rates**: Impacts purchasing power and monetary policy decisions.
- **Unemployment Rates**: Reflects labor market strength and consumer spending potential.

Market Indicators:

- **Stock Market Indexes**: Keep track of benchmarks like the S&P 500, NASDAQ, and Dow Jones Industrial Average.
- **Volatility Index (VIX)**: Known as the "fear gauge," this measures market volatility.
- **Bond Yields**: Movements in yields often predict economic slowdowns or growth.

Sector-Specific Trends:

- **Technology**: Monitor advancements in AI, blockchain, and green energy.
- **Healthcare**: Stay updated on innovations like biotech breakthroughs.
- **Consumer Discretionary**: Watch for shifts in consumer behavior and spending patterns.

4. Follow Global Market Trends

Global markets are interconnected, and events in one region can have ripple effects worldwide.

Stay informed about:

- **Geopolitical Events**: Wars, elections, and trade agreements can influence market sentiment.
- **Currency Movements**: Changes in exchange rates affect import/export businesses and multinational corporations.
- **Emerging Markets**: These often present high-growth opportunities but come with increased risks.
- **Global Supply Chains**: Monitor disruptions in industries like semiconductors, energy, and agriculture.

5. Develop Analytical Skills

Staying informed isn't just about consuming information—it's about understanding and interpreting it effectively.

Ways to improve analytical skills:

- **Learn Technical Analysis**: Study chart patterns, moving averages, and other tools to predict short-term price movements.
- **Master Fundamental Analysis**: Analyze financial statements, competitive advantages, and growth potential to assess a company's intrinsic value.

- **Use Investment Simulators**: Platforms like Investopedia's simulator or virtual trading accounts help you practice in a risk-free environment.
- **Stay Curious**: Always ask why a trend is happening, not just what is happening.

6. Join Communities and Networks

Engaging with others in the investment community helps you gain diverse perspectives and learn from shared experiences.

Benefits of joining communities:

- **Access to Expert Insights**: Learn directly from seasoned investors.
- **Discussion of Trends**: Engage in debates and discussions to challenge your assumptions.
- **Shared Resources**: Gain access to articles, books, and tools you might have missed.
- **Accountability**: Being part of a group keeps you motivated to continue learning.

Where to connect:

- **Forums**: Participate in discussions on platforms like Reddit (r/investing) or Quora.
- **Investment Clubs**: Join local or online clubs to collaborate on strategies.
- **Social Media**: Follow financial influencers and analysts on platforms like Twitter or LinkedIn.

7. Leverage Technology

Technology has made it easier than ever to stay informed about market trends.

Tools and apps:

- **News Aggregators**: Use apps like Flipboard or Feedly to consolidate financial news.
- **Market Alerts**: Set up notifications for stock movements or economic announcements through apps like Robinhood, E*TRADE, or Fidelity.
- **Portfolio Management Software**: Tools like Personal Capital or Mint help track and analyze your investments.
- **AI and Big Data**: Explore platforms that use AI to predict trends or suggest investments based on data analysis.

8. Learn from Market History

History often provides valuable lessons for interpreting current trends. While no two events are identical, patterns often emerge.

Key historical events to study:

- **The Great Depression (1929)**: Lessons on speculative bubbles and the dangers of over-leverage.
- **Dot-Com Bubble (2000)**: Understanding how hype can drive valuations beyond sustainable levels.

- **2008 Financial Crisis**: Insights into systemic risks and the importance of diversification.
- **COVID-19 Crash (2020)**: Lessons on market recovery and resilience during unprecedented times.

Studying these events helps you recognize warning signs and prepare for future crises.

9. Stay Open to New Strategies

As markets evolve, new strategies and opportunities emerge. Staying rigid in your approach can limit your success.

Ways to stay adaptable:

- **Experiment Cautiously**: Allocate a small portion of your portfolio to try new strategies.
- **Adopt Sustainable Practices**: ESG (Environmental, Social, Governance) investing is growing in popularity and profitability.
- **Embrace Passive Investing**: Index funds and ETFs offer low-cost, diversified options.
- **Learn Alternative Strategies**: Explore options trading, short selling, or dividend growth investing as your knowledge expands.

10. Avoid Information Overload

While staying informed is essential, too much information can be overwhelming and counterproductive.

How to stay focused:

- **Set Learning Goals**: Focus on mastering one topic at a time, such as a specific sector or analysis method.

- **Curate Sources**: Limit yourself to a handful of trusted resources to avoid conflicting advice.

- **Take Breaks**: Allow time to reflect and process what you've learned.

- **Prioritize Relevance**: Concentrate on trends and news that align with your investment strategy.

Conclusion

Continuous education about market trends is a lifelong commitment that pays dividends in the form of better investment decisions, reduced risk, and greater financial success. By leveraging diverse resources, developing analytical skills, and staying adaptable, you can navigate the complexities of the market with confidence.

Remember, the most successful investors are not necessarily the ones with the most money—they are the ones with the most knowledge. Stay curious, stay informed, and stay ahead.

Never Forget To **REVIEW OUR BOOK On Amazon**

www.ingramcontent.com/pod-product-compliance
Lightning Source LLC
Chambersburg PA
CBHW071026240526
45469CB00006BD/2109